# Two Tales of Crow and Sparrow

# Two Tales of Crow and Sparrow

## *A Freudian Folkloristic Essay on Caste and Untouchability*

**ALAN DUNDES**

ROWMAN & LITTLEFIELD PUBLISHERS, INC.
*Lanham • Boulder • New York • Oxford*

ROWMAN & LITTLEFIELD PUBLISHERS, INC.

Published in the United States of America
by Rowman & Littlefield Publishers, Inc.
4720 Boston Way, Lanham, Maryland 20706

12 Hid's Copse Road
Cummor Hill, Oxford OX2 9JJ, England

British Library Cataloguing in Publication Information Available

**Library of Congress Cataloging-in-Publication Data**

Dundes, Alan.
    Two tales of crow and sparrow : a freudian folkloristic essay on caste and
untouchability / Alan Dundes.
        p.    cm.
    Includes bibliographical references.
    ISBN 0-8476-8456-3 (cloth : alk. paper). — ISBN 0-8476-8457-1 (paper :
alk. paper)
    1. Caste—India. 2. Untouchables—India. 3. Psychoanalysis and folklore—
India.  I. Title.
DS422.C3D77              1997
305.5'122'0954—dc21                                              97-25277

ISBN 0-8476-8456-3 (cloth : alk. paper)
ISBN 0-8476-8457-1 (pbk. : alk. paper)

Printed in the United States of America

♾™ The paper used in this publication meets the minimum requirements of American
National Standard for Information Sciences—Permanence of Paper for Printed Library
Materials, ANSI Z39.48–1984.

This essay is dedicated to the memory of A. K. Ramanujan: poet, linguist, folklorist, Indologist for the world, but to me, fellow graduate student, dear lifelong friend, and the person who first aroused my curiosity about India.

"I regard untouchability as the greatest blot on Hinduism. . . . If we do not cleanse ourselves of this cursed untouchability, Hinduism and Hindus are bound to perish."

M. K. Gandhi, *Caste Must Go and the Sin of Untouchability* (Ahmedabad: Navajivan Press, 1964), pp. 21, 41.

# Contents

# Preface

This is an essay about India. Actually, it is an essay about caste in India, caste being the unique and dominant form of social organization in that vast country. More specifically, it is an essay about untouchability, a curious but nonetheless devastating fundamental aspect of caste, an aspect that has caused countless instances of human suffering and pain for millions of individuals for many centuries.

My point of departure consists of two separate and distinct Indic folktales, both involving the characters of a crow and a sparrow. As a folklorist, I am persuaded that folktales, like all folklore, offer a kind of autobiographical ethnography, a picture of a people painted by that people (as opposed to portraits drawn by so-called objective outside observers). In that sense, folklore offers a view of a culture from the inside-out instead of the outside-in. I hope to show that these two tales of crow and sparrow reveal clearly the underlying basis of untouchability in India.

Following the presentation of the two folktales and their analysis, I shall consider defecation habits and toilet training in some detail. The ethnographic data available will confirm the insights afforded by the two folktales, suggesting that there may be a logical or *psycho*logical connection between child-rearing techniques in India with special reference to toilet training and the longstanding tradition of untouchability. The thesis is, in part, that what cannot be touched is feces and that those who touch or who are touched by feces are untouchables. Food and feces, mouth and anus, must be kept separate—one eats with one's right hand and one uses the left hand to wipe one's anus after defecation.

   I shall also have something to say about the sacred cow and about sati (suttee) or widow burning, two other noteworthy problematic and enigmatic elements of Indic culture that have long puzzled Indologists. Finally, I shall briefly examine Gypsy culture in order to demonstrate both the antiquity and the remarkable tenacity of the folk belief complex that has resulted in the far-reaching practice of untouchability in India.

# Acknowledgments

As a non-Indologist or specialist in India, I have had to rely on the large ethnographic literature devoted to caste and untouchability for my data. I am truly indebted to many individuals who were kind enough to recommend possible sources in that literature. They include Burton Benedict, Gerry Berreman, Stuart Blackburn, Sarah Caldwell, Lawrence Cohen, Wendy Doniger, Marc Galanter, Pauline Kolenda, Stanley Kurtz, Adrian Mayer, Vijaya Nagarajan, Kirin Narayan, and Kirtana Thangavelu, among others. I must also express my gratitude to the participants in two Ford Foundation of India workshops in folkloristics held in Hyderabad and Mysore in 1988/1989 for providing numerous versions of "Crow and Sparrow" tales in response to my inquiry. I am most grateful to Nalini Bhonsle and her daughter, Dr. Neela Bhonsle Manley, both originally from Poona, for translating a Marathi tale of "Crow and Sparrow" written in archaic Marathi and included in the biography of Chakradhar, the thirteenth-century founder of the Mahanubhava sect of Hinduism.

In view of the undoubtedly controversial nature of my interpretation of untouchability, I am obliged to add the usual formulaic disclaimer to the effect that none of the above-mentioned individuals bear any responsibility for that interpretation. They may have given me valuable references, but I take full credit or blame for my reading of those references. Because I am not a professional student of India, I have elected to quote passages from many of the standard ethnographic accounts to support my arguments. I thought if I paraphrased the data, I might be accused of stacking the evidence in some way. This is why there are so many citations quoted in this essay. Because of the diversity of my sources, I have elected not to try to normalize the spellings and diacritics of words derived from Indian languages. Instead, I have respected the choices made by individual authors of passages cited.

Finally, I must thank Dean Birkenkamp, executive editor of Rowman & Littlefield, for his enthusiastic encouragement of this project and for his valuable suggestions. I also very much appreciate the assistance of folklorist Lisa Sherman in the final preparation of the manuscript for publication.

# Two Tales of Crow and Sparrow

## Caste

It is quite possible that more has been written about the nature of caste than any other form of human social organization. Whether this is so or not, it cannot be denied that the scholarship devoted to caste is incredibly voluminous. It would take several lifetimes to read all that has been published on the subject. One bibliography on caste in India (Gilbert 1948) lists nearly two thousand entries, and that does not even include books and articles published in the last half of the twentieth century. (For monographs and essays written between 1950 and 1959, see Damle 1961.)

I make no claim to have made much of a dent in what is available. Instead, I have tended to rely on the many valuable surveys of available caste literature. Among the best summaries of the theoretical speculations about caste are: Roy 1934:39-63; Srinivas et al., 1959; Hutton 1963; Murdoch 1977; Kolenda 1978; Klass 1980; Gould 1987; and Quigley 1993. For representative modern considerations of caste, see Raheja 1988a; and Dirks 1992. For a useful overview of the earlier scholarship including the thoughts of missionaries, professional orientalists, and government administrators, see Cohn 1968. See also Bandyopadhyay 1974. For a Marxist take on caste, see Sharma 1983 and Currie 1992. One of the most lucid and succinct accounts of the complexities of caste was written by an Indian anthropologist (Karve 1958, 1959).

Caste is not a native term in any of the many indigenous languages of India. Nor is it originally an English word. There seems to be widespread consensus that the term derived from a Portuguese word *casta,* meaning approximately race, breed, lineage. Thus, a *homen de boa casta*, a man of good family, was an appropriate idiomatic usage. The term was apparently first applied to India in the sixteenth century. Garcia de Orta wrote in 1563 that "no one changes from his father's trade and all those of the same caste of shoemakers are the same" (Hutton 1963:47). Caste may be cognate with the word *chaste,* which would signify a nuance of purity.

Caste has fascinated and puzzled European travelers and scholars ever since it was first encountered. "Of all the many strange things with which the European meets in India, the strangest is the Caste System" (Hill 1930:51). Yet it was also clear that caste was "the foundation and core of Indian civilization" (Dirks 1992:57). As one traveler in India was told in perhaps oversimplified terms: "Caste is Hinduism and Hinduism is Caste!" (Muehl 1950:185).

There are two different somewhat overlapping caste systems found in India. The first is the ideal, or normative, system, which consists of only four castes. This system, known as *Varna,* includes three that are "twice-born," and the lowest ranked one which is only "once-born." The "first" birth is one's natural physical natal experience; the "second" birth refers to an initiation ceremony wherein the individual receives a sacred thread. Only *Brahmans*, *Ksatriyas*, and *Vaisyas* were permitted to undergo the ritual of second birth. *Sudras*, the lowest of the four, and untouchables, were not. At the risk of oversimplifying, we can say that the Brahman is the priest, the Ksatriya is the ruler, noble, or warrior, the Vaisya is a commoner or ordinary householder, and the lowly Sudra is a servant. The *Laws of Manu* (10:4-5) provide textual authority for the Varna system: "The Brahmana, the Kshatriya and the Vaisya castes are the twice-born ones, but the fourth, the Sudra, has one birth only; there is no fifth caste" (Sharma 1989:401; cf. Doniger 1991: 234). Sudras might have been the lowest of the four varnas, but it was in theory forbidden to employ them "to carry the dead or to sweep filth, urine or the leavings of food" (Dutt 1968:140). Those polluting tasks were left for untouchables, a group apparently left off the Varna map.

The second caste system is based on a social organizational unit called *Jati*, a term derived from the root "*ja,*" to be born (Karve 1958:133). Jati refers to a "local system of ranked, hereditary and mainly endogamous groups, each associated with one or more traditional occupations, and all interdependent" (Srinivas 1984:153-154). In contrast to the finite number of Varnas, there are innumerable castes contained in the various Jati systems. The discrepancy between the standard semi-literary fourfold Varna system and the more common multitudinous Jati system pervades caste scholarship (Oldenberg 1920:207). Yet the combination of Varna and Jati systems that constitute caste in India is indeed one of the "corner stones of the civilization of India" (Bonnerjea 1931:49). (For a useful discussion of Varna and Jati, see Khare 1978).

The distinction between *Varna* and *Jati* is critical if one is interested in determining the number of castes in a particular locale. In Varna terms, there can be no more than four; in Jati terms, the number will vary with the particular place. One anthropological study in central India noted a village that had a total population in 1954 of 912 individuals who were divided into twenty-five castes (Mayer 1956:118). Another observer noted that, in the locality in which she lived, Pachperwa, there were "sixty-one different castes" (Emerson 1930:299). Although the hierarchical rankings of the four Varna castes are fairly constant, the internal rankings of Jati castes may vary from region to region, even from village to village (Chakravarti 1989:9). Ranking may be ascertained through transactional analysis, e.g., who accepts food or water from whom (Marriot 1959). In any event, "There are more than three thousand castes as against the four Varnas prescribed in the Vedas" (Rao 1989:63).

We may now briefly consider two formal definitions of caste:

> A caste may be defined as an endogamous and hereditary subdivision of an ethnic unit occupying a position of superior or inferior rank or social esteem in comparison with other such subdivisions. . . . Actually the census of India records over eight hundred castes and subcastes, or nearly five thousand, counting minute or wholly localized ones. These include not only occupational groups but tribes, races, sects, in fact all populational bodies possessing any distinctive traits and group consciousness. (Kroeber 1930:254,255)

The second definition was written by a specialist in India:

> The term "caste" has been widely used to describe ranked groups within rigid systems of social stratification and especially those which constitute the society of Hindu India . . . . A caste might . . . be defined as a network of status equal interactions in a society characterized by a network of hierarchical interactions between birth-ascribed groups. (Berreman 1968:333-334)

One bone of contention about caste is whether the term, in the strict sense, applies exclusively to the system of social inequality found in India or whether it can be applied cross-culturally in a looser sense to any social system marked by inequality (cf. Pitt Rivers 1971 and Pandey 1986:38-39, nos. 3-4 concerning this debate). The issue really turns on whether one is primarily interested in similarities or differences between cultures. My own position is that the caste system, as it is found in India with its particular constellation of distinctive features, is unique.

Another area of dispute concerns the possible or likely origins of caste. Some have argued that there are racial or ethnic origins; others claim that occupations determine caste affiliation. Most of these arguments are highly speculative and are at best inconclusive. Earlier discussion of "origins" of caste have yielded to more empirical examinations of the function and structure of caste, not to mention political activists seeking to minimize the deleterious effects of caste upon those unfortunate enough to occupy the lower ranks in the caste system. But whatever the theory of origin proposed or the functionalist or structuralist description offered, no convincing explanation has yet been proposed that has succeeded in illuminating all the "curious rules about purity and impurity of certain kinds of foods or of the restrictions about taking food of a particular kind from others" (Chattopadhyay 1925:349).

Certainly the rigidity and hierarchical nature of the caste system in India are indisputable. Since caste membership is ascribed by birth, there is little or no chance for upward mobility. In a village in western Orissa, we learn that "In the streets of the clean castes one never finds a man cutting hair who is not of *barber* caste, nor a woman sweeping the street who is not of *barber* caste, nor a washerman who is not also of the *washerman* caste" (Bailey 1957:95).

All castes, with the possible exception of the Brahmans, felt they had some castes above them and some below them. As one Marathi poet (Govindaraj) phrased it: Hindu society is made up of men "who bow their head to the kicks from above, who simultaneously give a kick below, never thinking to resist the one or refrain from the other" (Karve 1959:157). This is true even of the lower-ranked castes. "There is no caste in India so low that it does not find another one that in their own eyes is still inferior" (Fuchs 1981:207). For example, "among those lowest scavenging sections which remove nightsoil there is still a distinction: those who serve in private houses consider themselves higher than those who clean public latrines" (Fuchs 1981:238). The point here is that even among the untouchables, there are hierarchical gradations whereby one caste feels superior or inferior to another.

A reader unfamiliar with India and who is imbued with the modern Western ideals of egalitarianism and the possibility of upward social mobility in a system that rewards *achieved* status as opposed to *ascribed* status may wonder why individuals "trapped" in low-ranked castes do not try to escape their lifelong position of culturally defined inferiority. The answer lies in the fact that the caste system is closely connected to worldview and religious belief. For example, the idea of rebirth, reincarnation as part of an elaborate system of eschatology, allows an individual to ponder upward mobility in the next life. Milner has argued persuasively that the "near endless mobility" possible in future lives is a kind of "structural reversal" of the "prohibition against mobility in the caste system" (1993:301). As Milner aptly put it: "The key principle of the worldly system is no mobility; the key principle of the otherworldly system is endless mobility" (1993:304). An untouchable in his autobiography recalled his grandmother's soothing words of solace:

> . . . she would tell me that we were Untouchables only for one life, and that after this life we would be born either as a high-caste Hindu or a prince. This present life, she explained, was only the curse of the sins which we had committed in our past life, and all human beings have to go through this wheel of Karma, but if we were willing to do our work and be subjected to the discomforts of this world we should have reward in the next life. (Hazari 1951:31)

To understand this worldview, one must appreciate the concept of *Karma*. The idea is that after death, the soul may be reborn again and again. This process of rebirth "is governed by a law of *Karma* which is a law of nature." According to this law, "every action automatically produces inevitable rewards or punishments which become operative in the future." Further, "the social caste into which one is born is the necessary effect of these accumulating rewards and punishments" (Taylor 1948:6). One cannot legitimately protest against one's fate since in theory, one's fate was caused by one's own actions in a previous life. "Rebelling against one's lot involves both disrespect for the law of *Karma* and failure to do one's proper duties, and on both grounds have the necessary result of making one's *Karma* worse, and so producing a regression to a lower stage in the next birth" (Taylor 1948:7). If one accepts this notion of Karma, then one becomes resigned to one's place in life (Taylor 1948:9). So not only would it be futile to try to escape from one's birth-ascribed caste affiliation, but the very act of trying to escape would likely result in even a lower-ranked caste membership in one's next life. The idea that one's lot in life was "caused" by actions in one's previous life is critical. Thus, if one is of a lower caste or an untouchable, it is presumably because of some sin of omission or commission, e.g., involving pollution in a previous life. This kind of fatalistic, deterministic thinking tends to make individuals more or less accepting of—though not necessarily content with—their caste assignment.

So far we have discussed caste's rigid hierarchy with rank determined in part by birth, but what precisely is it that makes one caste outrank another and keeps the castes separate? Many writers on the subject have recognized that the whole concept of caste is inextricably tied up with some kind of native category of defilement or pollution. Hocart remarked, for instance:

> The conclusion we have arrived at on modern evidence is that the caste system is a sacrificial organization, that the aristocracy are feudal lords constantly involved in rites for which they require vassals or serfs, because some of these services involve pollution from which the lord must remain free. (1968:17)

This view is similar to anthropologist Nadel's observation that "the whole caste system revolves upon the existence of the lower castes. For a human being of such perfection as the Brahman is conceived to be is barred from hundreds of lowly tasks which are yet necessary for his existence. He must have cleanliness, but he is not permitted to sweep. . . ." (1954:17). A traveler in India saw evidence of this:

> Enroute we passed through a Brahman village, the first one I had seen inhabited by just one caste. It was unutterably filthy, for there was no one to see to the thousand petty tasks proscribed to the Brahmins. Its people lived aloof in the most awful squalor rather than lowering themselves to cleaning their own dooryards. (Muehl 1950:175)

Many anthropologists and specialists on India have remarked on the critical importance of pollution to the caste system. It has been called the "chief principle" upon which the entire caste system depends (Stevenson 1954:46). Ketkar said this in his *History of Caste in India*, first published in 1909 (1979:121). Hanumanthan, who wrote a history of untouchability, remarked that "the fundamental notions of purity and impurity" form "the basis of the rigid caste system and untouchability" (1979:173). Mandelbaum noted that the basic organizing principles of caste included "the stress of endogamy," "hierarchical social order," and "the social consequences of ritual pollution and purity" (1959:145). Srinivas, a leading Indian anthropologist, has stated: "It is impossible to detach Hinduism from the caste system. . . . Certain ideas regarding pollution and purity are cardinal to Hinduism" (1962:150,151). To be sure, there are some writers who consider "purity-pollution" to be secondary rather than primary, claiming that it was "not the cause of untouchability but its effect" (Sheth 1990:596). Similarly, sociologist Murray Milner contends that pollution is merely a metaphor to symbolize status differences. Pollution permits the expression of concern about social interaction between those "who are unequal in status" and that purity and pollution must *not* be made "the fundamental analytical category for understanding caste" (1994: 110-111, 115; cf. Marglin 1977:265).

Nevertheless, there is agreement that it is the ranking of castes that appears to be determined by degrees of purity or pollution. Marriott, another authority on India, articulated the matter this way: "A Caste is said to be considered high if its characteristic way of life is judged to be high and pure, or low if its way of life is judged to be low and polluted" (1959:92). If we subtract the circular elements of the definition (using "high" and "low" within the definition itself) we are left with "pure" versus "polluted." Davis has summarized the issue well:

> . . . impurity is marked by involvement with life processes (such as birth and death) and life substances (including the effluvia of the human body: hair, sweat, blood, semen, feces, urine, and rheum of the eyes, for example). Purity is marked by the lack of involvement with such processes and substances. Rank is then said to be determined by relative degrees of purity and impurity. The greater the purity, the higher the rank. The lesser the purity, the lower the rank. (1976:16)

Anthropologist F. G. Bailey even went so far as to speak of a "barrier of pollution," noting that untouchables cannot better themselves "because they are on the wrong side of the barrier of pollution"

(1957:226). At this point, the importance of pollution in the definition of caste is no longer debated. Harper's 1964 essay, "Ritual Pollution as an Integrator of Caste and Religion," as well as Louis Dumont's seminal *Homo Hierarchicus*, first published in French in 1966, which is arguably the single most influential book on caste ever written, further document the dependence of the caste system on the concept of pollution. For Dumont, the fundamental "single true principle" underlying caste in India is "the opposition of the pure and the impure" (1980:43).

It must be said that not all Indologists agree with Dumont's "single true principle" as the basis of caste (cf. Barnett et al. 1976). In a review of Dumont by Das and Uberoi, it is claimed that "It is not the opposition between the pure and the impure . . . that makes up the elementary structure of the caste system" (1971:41). In a similar argument, Raheja contended that auspiciousness and inauspiciousness are more critical in caste hierarchical relationships than "the simple opposition of the pure and impure" (1988b:27-28). Auspiciousness and inauspiciousness may be roughly defined in terms of good luck/fortune and bad luck/fortune. In Raheja's scheme, inauspiciousness (or disease) can be avoided or transferred through a ritual gift (*dän*). The theoretical problem with Raheja's attempt to displace Dumont's pure/impure thesis is that good luck/bad luck occur presumably in all human societies in some form or other; caste and untouchability, in contrast, do not! The magical transference of disease, for example, is a very common folkloristic phenomenon (cf. Hand 1965). The technique is widespread in India. "In the Punjab when near relations of a new-born babe come to see him for the first time, they encircle a one-rupee note around him, which is then given away to the scavenger. This is not done to remove any impurity, but is said to protect the new-born from the evil eye" (Das and Uberoi 1971:37-38). Clearly this apotropaic measure designed to ward off the evil eye is separate and distinct from the matter of impurity. In fairness, it should be noted that Raheja is well aware of the difference between her scheme and Dumont's. "First, impurity cannot be removed through any sort of transferral to a recipient, as inauspiciousness is removed through the giving of *dän*. . . . Second, forms of impurity have little if any relevance for more generalized well-being or auspiciousness" (1988b:46). Those Indologists who believe that somehow Raheja's scheme has made Dumont's emphasis on pure/impure obsolete are very much mistaken. It may well be that both dichotomies are germane to Indian culture, but there is no evidence to support the notion that the "auspiciousness" model has made the Dumont thesis passé. I shall try to show that Dumont was correct in underlining the importance of purity and pollution, but that he did not go nearly far enough in analyzing the rationale of that critical dichotomy.

I have taken pains to quote the above authorities on caste to show precisely what the state of our knowledge on the subject is. I have done this because I intend to suggest that while these views are not really wrong, they are inadequate and incomplete. The question remains: if purity and pollution are so central to caste, what exactly is it that determines whether an object, an act, or a person is polluted or polluting? In sum, is there perhaps an unconscious folk belief complex which would explain the curious form of social organization called caste?

Before moving on to untouchability, let us briefly review the salient features of caste.

1. There is a vertical hierarchical grouping of castes in any one locale—the highest the Brahman and the lowest the untouchables (cf. Pohlman 1951:376).
2. Caste membership is ascribed rather than achieved, and the ascription is determined by birth.
3. Castes tend to be endogamous such that intermarriage between castes is strongly discouraged.
4. Castes are often (though not always) associated with specific traditional occupations.
5. Castes are ranked on the basis of pollution or the relative absence thereof. Brahmans are the most pure; untouchables are the most polluted.
6. Caste purity (hence status) can be negatively altered through direct or indirect physical contact with a member of a lower caste, e.g., through accepting food or water from such an individual.
7. Temporary defilement or pollution can be alleviated or eliminated by bathing, changing clothes, or some ritual procedure, but a serious defiling act can result in permanent expulsion from the caste (producing individuals who become *outcastes*).

## Untouchability

Of all the various aspects of caste, untouchability is surely the most perplexing and, if I may be permitted a value judgment, the most horrifying. Why should any group or class of individuals in a society be deemed *untouchable*? And to the extent that physical contact with such an individual should require immediate rituals of purification? It is this basic question which has provided the primary impetus for the present essay. I do not believe that to date any convincing explanation for this practice has been offered by anthropologist or Indologist. It has been *described* in detail, but not *analyzed* or *explained*!

One study of the subject begins, "untouchability is one of the most acute problems in India. It is also a problem which is unique to India. It is nowhere found in the same form as it is found in this country" (Mohapatra and Mohanty 1973-1974:18; for dozens of references on the subject, see Zelliot, 1972). Another writer makes a similar claim: "Untouchability is a unique Hindu social institution" (Kshirsagar 1986:9). There are those who have argued that untouchability, like the larger category caste, is *not* unique to India, but rather has analogues in other societies, e.g., in Japan and in Korea (cf. Passin 1955, Chakravarti and Subedi 1995). However, I am convinced that untouchability in the form that is found throughout India with its indubitable connection with the entire complex caste system is not replicated anywhere else in the world—except where immigrants from India have settled.

It is one thing to say that "untouchability is a cardinal feature of the caste system" (Ramu 1968:147); it is quite another to define untouchability satisfactorily. One writer has suggested that "untouchability in the sense of physical contact is the crux of untouchability" (Desai 1976:257).

Dubois's succinct account of untouchability is as apt as any (1906:51):

> Anyone who has been touched, whether inadvertently or purposely, by a Pariah is defiled by that single act, and may hold no communication with any person whatsoever until he has been purified by bathing, or by other ceremonies more or less important according to the status and customs of his caste. It would be contamination to eat with any members of this class; to touch food prepared by them, or even to drink water which they have drawn; to use an earthen vessel which they have held in their hands; to set foot inside one of their houses, or to allow them to enter houses other than their own. Each of these acts would contaminate the person affected by it, and

before being readmitted to his own caste such a person would
have to go through many exacting and expensive formalities.

(For details of the life of French missionary Jean-Antoine Dubois
(1766-1848) whose ethnographic magnum opus *Hindu Manners, Customs
and Ceremonies* was based upon intensive fieldwork carried out at the
end of the eighteenth century in south India, see Hockings 1977.)

One very important distinction that cannot be stressed enough is
the difference between the state of pollution of a caste member caused by
contact with a lower caste member, e.g., an untouchable, and the actual
status of untouchability. Contamination or pollution can be undone or
removed, as Dubois's account suggests. It is thus only *temporary*
defilement. In contrast, an untouchable "is born an untouchable, he
carries the disability to the grave and no expiatory ceremony will enable
him to get rid of it. Moreover, the defilement becomes hereditary and is
bequeathed to his children" (Hanumanthan 1979:8). Untouchability is
based on birth and occupation (Sorabji 1933:701). Untouchability, in this
sense, is permanent, not temporary. I intend to demonstrate, however,
that both temporary and permanent defilement stem from the same basic
psychological causative factors. (For a discussion of the distinction
between temporary and permanent pollution, see Stevenson 1954:50;
Khare 1962:126; Jha 1975:24.)

It is the feature of absolute permanency of defilement that may
be difficult for Westerners to grasp. As mentioned above, there is
virtually no opportunity for social mobility and, moreover, those living
in the system tend to accept their birth-produced status. They may not
like it, but they are resigned to it. As one group of untouchables phrased
it: "About their birth in Yoleya caste, they say it is God's will; 'we do
not have a say about our birth; we cannot plan our birth, thus we have
to suffer mutely.' A few of them consider that 'it is owing to the sin
committed in the previous birth, that the punishment is given in this
life'" (Ramu 1968:152). This would appear to be a folk articulation of
the Karma principle (cf. Gandhi 1982-1983:259).

Untouchables are known by a number of different euphemistic
labels: Depressed Classes, Outcastes, Pariahs (Fuchs 1981:2). For a
historical discussion of the term *untouchable*, see Charsley 1966. Perhaps
most common is "Scheduled Castes," or the term proposed by Mahatma
Gandhi, "Harijans," meaning "Children of God." But no matter what the
term of preference might be, Brahmans and other so-called high castes

were obsessively afraid of being polluted or defiled by the touch of an untouchable. For this reason, untouchables were not permitted access to restaurants, hotels, or even temples. They were not allowed to draw water from public wells—even if the public well was the only water source available in a particular village. They were typically forced to live in segregated housing, and were not given an opportunity to attend public school or participate in any political process or to own land. These admittedly are the extreme forms of proscriptive rules that governed the lives of untouchables, but some examples of these rules continue unabated—if sometimes attenuated—in India at the beginning of the twenty-first century.

Let me present several representative examples of incredible restrictions that have prevailed for centuries in regard to untouchables.

> In Maratha country a Mahar might not spit on the road lest a caste Hindu might get polluted by touching it. To save those people from pollution, the Mahar had to carry an earthen spittoon, hung from his neck, in which he was to spit. Further he had to drag a thorny branch with him to wipe out his footprints and to lie at a distance prostrate on the ground if a Brahman passed by, so that his foul shadow might not defile the Brahman. (Kundu 1983: 273; cf. Briggs 1953:124, and Kamble 1982:35)

Similar descriptions abound elsewhere in India. Speaking of untouchable practices in days gone by in Gujurat, Stevenson remarks (1930:2-3):

> Yet in the old days our friend would have had to place a stag's horn in his turban, that all might be warned not to touch him; to wear a spittoon in front of him lest his spittle should pollute the earth; and to drag thorns behind him that his footprints might be effaced, and the soil not defiled for a proud Brahman's tread. (cf. Fuchs 1981:180)

Strange as it may seem, lower-caste members were required to keep a definite respectable distance from members of higher-ranking castes, distances given in specific measure. Depending upon the relationship prevailing between the two castes involved, the distance in question could vary from 24 feet to 36 feet to 64 feet (Kamble 1982:35). Consider the following typical account of the social distance requirements: "There is even a scale of distances within which different Panchamas as the untouchables are called in South India, may not approach Brahmans, e.g., eight yards for Kammalans, twelve yards for Iluvans or Tiyans, sixteen yards for Pulayans, thirty-two yards from the Paraiyans or Pariahs" (O'Malley 1932:141; cf. Hutton 1963:80 for other examples).

Untouchables were expected to call out or make some noise to signal their presence and location so that high castes could avoid them. Novelist Anand paints a picture of what happens when an untouchable unintentionally bumps into a high-caste person on the street:

> "Keep to the side of the road, you low-caste vermin!" he suddenly heard someone shouting at him. "Why don't you call, you swine, and announce your approach! Do you know you have touched me and defiled me, you cock-eyed son of a bow-legged scorpion! Now I will have to go and take a bath to purify myself. And it was a new dhoti and shirt I put on this morning!" (Anand 1986:46)

The fear of being polluted by the "outside world" was a constant one among Brahmans and other high-caste individuals. Indian anthropologist Karve reports the following personal reminiscence: "The author, a Brahman, remembers that as a school girl she had to change all her school-clothes which were polluted through coming in contact with 'God knows what castes', before being allowed to eat or move freely in the house" (Karve 1958:157). This corresponds closely with what a South Malabar child was told: "You must always bathe before touching any of the older people when you return from school" (Mencher 1963:56). It is noteworthy that sometimes defiled caste members bathed with their clothes on—as if the clothing had to be cleaned as well. "When a caste man becomes unclean by touching a dog or a Candala . . . under such circumstances, he must bathe with his clothes on" (Briggs 1953:30).

The bathing requirement reminds us of the whole issue of obtaining clean water, that is, "clean" in a ritual sense. It may be difficult for Westerners to imagine an untouchable prohibited from drawing water from the community well, waiting patiently, sometimes for hours at a time, for some passing individual to take pity on him or her, and to pour some water from their "clean" container into their "unclean" one. Here we are not talking necessarily about water for bathing but water for drinking or cooking as well. The untouchable "must just stand humbly by and wait till some member of a high caste of his charity draws water and pours it into this Untouchable's water-vessel. Even the charitable would take extraordinary care not to come into contact with the Dhed or his water-vessel, but would raise his own pot and pour the water from some height above" (Stevenson 1930:3). "In practice no one drinks out of a vessel belonging to anyone of another caste. It would be legitimate to do so if the owner of the vessel belonged to a higher caste, but the latter would not allow it as his vessel would be defiled by the lips of a man of lower caste. There is not the same objection however to a man drinking water poured into his cupped hands from another man's vessel, which in this way is kept free from taint" (O'Malley 1932:109-110).

This technique is evidently of considerable antiquity. None other than Marco Polo described it in detail near the end of the thirteenth century. The ethnographic passage in question begins with his observation in India of a left-right hand distinction.

> It ought to be noticed, that in eating they make use of the right hand only, nor do they ever touch food with the left. For every cleanly and delicate work they employ the former, and reserve the latter for the base uses of personal abstersion, and other offices connected with the animal functions. They drink out of a particular kind of vessel, and each individual from his own, never making use of the drinking pot of another person. When they drink they do not apply the vessel to the mouth, but hold it above the head, and pour the liquor into the mouth, not suffering the vessel on any account to touch the lips. In giving drink to a stranger, they do not hand their vessel to him, but, if he is not provided with one of his own, pour the wine or other liquor into his hands, from which he drinks it, as from a cup. (Polo 1961:341)

Marco Polo does not mention the term *untouchable* but his description nonetheless certainly rings true.

In Anand's classic novel, *Untouchable*, first published in 1935, we have a finely drawn painful portrait of untouchables seeking water:

> The outcastes were not allowed to mount the platform surrounding the well, because if they were ever to draw water from it, the Hindus of the three upper castes would consider the water polluted. Nor were they allowed to access to the

near-by brook as their use of it would contaminate the stream. They had no well of their own because it cost at least a thousand rupees to dig a well. . . . Perforce they had to collect at the foot of the caste Hindus' well and depend on the bounty of some of their superiors to pour water into their pitchers. More often than not there was no caste Hindu present. . . . So the outcastes had to wait for chance to bring some caste Hindu to the well, for luck to decide that he was kind, for Fate to ordain that he had time—to get their pitchers filled with water. They crowded round the well, congested the space below its high brick platform, morning, noon and night, joining their hands with servile humility to every passer-by, cursing their fate, and bemoaning their lot, if they were refused the help they wanted, praying, beseeching and blessing, if some generous soul condescended to listen to them, or to help them. (Anand 1986:22-23)

Getting a drink of water from a well or a fountain is an act which is taken for granted in most of the world, but not in India for an untouchable!

It is not my purpose to document all the hardship and, from an ethnocentric point of view, needless pain caused to thousands upon thousands of individuals over the centuries by the practice of untouchability. The restriction against drawing water from public wells is just one tiny example of the problem (Srinivas and Béteille 1965:14). Consider the following cruel account reported in 1913:

Not long ago, at Kohat, nestling on the border of Afghanistan, the two-year-old son of a well-to-do Hindu fell into a well. The cries of the panic-stricken ladies of the family attracted the attention of a man who was cleaning the street outside. He immediately rushed to the spot and volunteered to go down into the well and bring up the boy. Although no other male was within hearing, and no female was willing to jeopardize her life in the attempt to rescue the little fellow, the 'sweeper' was not permitted to save the child, since, being 'untouchable,' his 'touch' would pollute the water. By the time a man belonging to a higher caste could be brought to the scene of the accident, the poor boy was drowned. (Singh 1913:376; for more contemporary incidents, see Sharma 1983:73-75)

There are many other anecdotal illustrations of a "death before dishonor" in connection with accepting water from the hands of an untouchable. In *Indian Caste Customs*, we are told that:

> St. James's Church in Delhi was built by Col. James Skinner in fulfillment of a vow which he made while lying wounded on a battle-field. He had been left there for dead and lay for two nights and a day suffering agonies from thirst and the pain of his wound. Near him lay a Rajput officer who had lost a leg. A Chamar, who is an untouchable, came along with water, which Skinner drank; but the Rajput refused, saying that he would rather die than be defiled; and he consequently died. (O'Malley 1932:110-111)

Temple entry is yet another part of the untouchability constellation of traits. Just as high-caste members can be contaminated by touch or by an untouchable's entering their residence, so evidently are gods and their icons equally susceptible to contamination, and so also are their dwellings, namely temples. The rules governing access to temples are strict. "Not all caste men may approach the god himself, or enter the inner sanctuary. There are degrees even of private entrée—so many feet away from a worshipper of such and such a caste" (Sorabji 1933:691).

The central character in Anand's novel, *Untouchable*, wishes to enter a temple. "But he hadn't the courage to go. He felt weak. He realized that an Untouchable going into a temple polluted it past purification" (1986:58). Then gathering his courage, he mounts the external steps leading to the temple entrance. As he peered into the temple, a shout rings out "Polluted, polluted, polluted," "The distance, the distance!" the worshippers from the top of the stairs were shouting. A temple can be polluted according to the Holy Books by a low-caste man coming within sixty-nine yards of it, and here he was actually on the steps, at the door. "We are ruined. We will need to have a sacrificial fire in order to purify ourselves and our shrine" (Anand 1983:62).

Even holy men were subject to the rules of untouchables. For example, there was once a saint of Maharashtra who was a Mahar, an untouchable caste, who was "a great devotee of the god Vithoba of Pandharpur. He worshipped this god standing outside the temple because as an untouchable he was not allowed to go into the temple" (Karve 1959: 153). It is easy to understand in this context why virtually the only converts to Christianity in India came from the ranks of the untouchables who welcomed its egalitarianism and the unquestioned right to enter churches freely. On the other hand, missionaries who accepted untouchables into their congregations did not realize that the presence of former untouchables automatically precluded the possibility of higher-caste members from joining that same congregation (cf. Wiser and Wiser 1971:55).

Untouchables were also kept out of schools, shops, and hotels, among other public arenas (for hotel instances, see Sagar 1975, and Khan 1980:153-157). The daily indignities and humiliations are impossible to measure. We do have occasional reports from untouchables. According to one such informant: "One feels one's Untouchability most of the time. I've never shared a meal with caste Hindus and I would never draw water from their well. . . . My father used to warn me not to let my shadow fall on a Brahman. . . . I certainly wouldn't go into the house of one unless invited and I've noticed how sometimes they spray water in my path before I enter. It's insulting, but something one gets used to" (Baker 1990:153).

The school situation was especially poignant. "The villagers never forgot, nor did they let us forget, that we were untouchables. High-caste children sat inside the school; the Bauri children, about twenty of us, sat outside on the veranda and listened. The two teachers, a Brahman outsider, and a temple servant, refused to touch us, even with a stick. To beat us, they threw bamboo canes. The higher-caste children threw mud at us. Fearing severe beatings, we dared not fight back" (Freeman 1979:67). In another account of school restrictions, "But the masters wouldn't teach the outcastes, lest their fingers which guided the students across the text should touch the leaves of the outcastes' books and they be polluted" (Anand 1986:39). I suppose that at least untouchability prevented sadistic teachers from laying hands on untouchable students. There are surely not many advantages of being an untouchable. However, in western Orissa, "by tradition the village watchmen are always *outcastes*. This policy was rationalized by an early British official on the grounds that the touch of an *outcaste* pollutes and therefore he can discipline people simply by threatening to touch them" (Bailey 1957:149).

The threat of touch is credible in the light of an Indian anthropologist's account of a holy man returning from a bath in the Ganges. He met an untouchable "who suddenly moved forward and was about to touch him. . . . He asked the intruder to stop advancing and go away at once without polluting him" (Saraswati 1987:20). The untouchable laughed and posed a series of questions: "Whom you want to go? Me or my body? My body, or my shadow? How is my shadow different from yours? How is my body different from yours?" (Saraswati 1987:21). The holy man realized the glaring discrepancy between what he preached and what he practiced. "But before he could speak a word of apology, the stranger vanished." The untouchable "was no less than god Shiva himself in disguise." The point is that the holy man was not afraid of being robbed or hurt, just of being polluted by the touch of an untouchable.

Occasionally, the threat of touch could be utilized for economic advantage. It is reported (Searle-Chatterjee 1979:281) that if a high-caste individual entered an area inhabited by untouchable sweepers, they might surround him and "touch him until he gave them money to be rid of them."

Because the untouchable was "debarred from using all public conveniences, roads, vehicles, ferries, wells, schools, restaurants, and tea shops" (Fuchs 1981:4), the most elementary activity was invariably fraught with personal peril. An untouchable "making a purchase from a shopkeeper has to go through a long and humiliating process. He places money on the ground in front of the shop and withdraws to a safe distance. The shopkeeper then comes out with the goods, puts them on the ground, and takes up the money. The Panchama finally advances after the shopkeeper is back in his shop and removes his purchases" (O'Malley 1932:142). In a village in western Orissa, a similar experience was the rule. "Physical contact alone is what matters. If money or other small things are passing between persons in clean and unclean categories, then one party cups his hands and other drops the object into them. In other cases the object is laid on the ground to be picked up by the other party" (Bailey 1957:213-214). Hazari, author of an untouchable autobiography, reports (1951:63): "The shopkeepers still threw goods I bought, either into my basket or the piece of cloth which I might carry for that purpose." One individual brought up in Bombay remembered what happened when he went back to his family's village in Gujerat: "When you paid a shopkeeper, he would give you your change by dropping it in your shirt that you had to hold out to catch it. It was a humiliating thing" (Isaacs 1965:62). In this context, it is interesting to recall one small incident of social protest. Once in a street fair in the Punjab, the sweepers set up a booth bearing the sign, "This shop is exclusively for 'untouchables.' No 'touchable' will be served" (Singh

1913:384).

Probably the largest set of caste restrictions had to do with the taking of food from a lower caste. It is this prohibition more than any other that accounts for the fact that a great many cooks in India are Brahmans, the logic being that all castes can take/eat food prepared by Brahmans (Wolpert 1991:120). That is why "Brahmans are also employed as cooks in jails, so that caste susceptibilities cannot be offended" (O'Malley 1932:105). Similar reasoning explains why Brahmans were "employed to supply water to thirsty railway passengers by pouring it into their cupped hands, cups, or other vessels" (O'Malley 1932:110). "And the traveller in India may at any railway station hall, throughout the country, hear the cry, 'I'm a Brahman; I water all castes.'" (Sorabji 1933:692).

In those cases where Brahman cooks serve "masters" from lower castes, these masters cannot touch the pots that their cook uses in preparing their food. "The cook will serve the food when it is ready, but not remove what is left after the meal is over. What the Brahman cook prepares and touches is pure for his master, but what the master touches is impure and would defile the cook" (Dubois 1906:293). One must keep in mind that "No member of a Hindu caste may accept cooked food, salt, milk or water from an untouchable. His touch is polluting, even his nearness is often sufficient to defile a man of high caste" (Fuchs 1981:4).

This is just a small sampling of the restrictions imposed upon untouchables. There are many, many more. For example, a tailor in rural Gujurat may not take measurements by touching an untouchable. Instead, "He guesses the measurements or gives the tape to the untouchable and notes approximately the measurements" (Desai 1976:132).

I want to remind the reader that whereas high-caste individuals can usually undo the allegedly defiling effects of contact with an untouchable, untouchables themselves have no recourse to "undoing" their status as untouchables. This refers to the distinction between temporary and permanent defilement noted previously. Naipaul reported a striking example of the ironclad immutability of caste untouchability. A foreign businessman impressed with an intelligent "untouchable" servant decided to educate him, and so, before he left the country, he placed him in a better job. Upon returning to India some years later, the businessman found that "his untouchable was a latrine-cleaner again" (Naipaul 1977:188). His clan had boycotted him for breaking away from them. He could not join any other group; there was no woman he could marry. He had become marginalized and had no choice other than returning to his "duty." The obvious moral: once a latrine-cleaner, always a latrine-cleaner!

One might well imagine that untouchables having been subjected to such a wide gamut of indignities would be unwilling to practice any form of untouchability themselves. But such is not the case. There are different untouchable castes, and they, like all other Indian castes, perceive themselves in some kind of rank order vis-à-vis other untouchable castes. One writer has described this form of the Indian pecking order as follows:

> But what has been most insanely tragic in the practice of untouchability is its prevalence in no less acute a form even among the untouchables themselves. . . . It must not be forgotten that the untouchables in India do not belong to any particular low caste. They are members of a vast and sprawling federation of low castes throughout India. This division of the Sudras into a rigid system of small fragments of low-castes had brought in its train the display of the same degree of social cruelties to the unlucky lowest-caste untouchables by the slightly higher-caste untouchables as was shown to the whole federation of untouchables by the high-caste Hindus. To the high-caste untouchables hatred for the lower order untouchables acted as a sort of anodyne. This would lessen the burden of their own pain by transferring their anger to the lower-order untouchables, who in their turn could not retaliate. (Das 1985:300, cf. the chapter "Untouchability among the Untouchables Themselves" in Desai 1976:39-50, and Kadetotad 1966)

There are evidently degrees of untouchability. "Eleven castes will not touch a Bhangi, seventeen will not touch a Chamar, ten will not touch a Dharkar, sixteen will not touch a Dhobi or a Dom" (Blunt 1931:102). Each caste has a different degree of potential contamination and furthermore the ranking can vary from region to region. Consider one definition of the position of Chamars who are "tanners of leather, preparers of skins, manufacturers of leather articles, and makers of shoes." From distinctions made in the Census Report for 1901, Briggs (1920:1, 19-20) remarks:

> Certain castes which fall below the twice-born were grouped as follows: Those from whose hands Brahmans will take

> water; those from whose hands some of the higher castes will
> take water; those from whom the twice-born cannot take wa-
> ter, but who are not untouchable; those whose touch defiles,
> but do not eat beef; and those who eat beef and vermin and
> whose touch defiles. In this last class the Chamar belongs.

Many of the village investigations of caste have been greatly concerned with determining the "exact" rank order of all the castes in the local population as well as the criteria for that ranking.

The desperate plight of the untouchables is not just a matter of inconvenience or occasional humiliation. It is sometimes a matter of life and death. Not only were untouchables not permitted to draw water from public wells, but their own wells were often despoiled. Higher-caste oppressors would "throw excreta into their drinking water wells; polluting their wells by throwing into them filth, dead dogs, cats and bones of animals" (Kamble 1982:46). There was also the distinct possibility of physical harassment, e.g., being burned alive (Kamble 1982:40; Baker 1990:57). Much of the literature devoted to untouchability consists of the documentation of the various atrocities untouchables have endured (cf. Hanumanthan 1979:225-232).

The reader may well wonder how many untouchables there are in India. Is it a matter of just several thousand unfortunate souls forced to live out their lives under the unalterable yoke of this denigrating and degrading social system? According to the 1961 census, there were 65 million untouchables (Sharma 1974:305; cf. Lambert 1958:57), but one must remember that population rates of growth in India are quite extraordinary. The 1981 census listed 105 million untouchables (Deliège 1992:155). One source claims there are 1106 major untouchable castes in India (Kamble 1982:2). Whatever the precise number of untouchables, it is clear that we are talking about a considerable number of individuals.

Another question that logically arises concerns whether or not there has been any systematic attempt by the government of India or any advocacy group to abolish untouchability. Not too long after India's independence in 1947, Article 17 of the Constitution, which became the law of the land in 1950, declared:

"Untouchability is abolished and its practice in any form is forbidden. The enforcement of any disability arising out of Untouchability shall be an offense punishable in accordance with law" (Aggarwal and Ashraf 1976:35; Mohapatra and Mohanty 1973-1974:19). But it is not easy to legislate such a practice out of existence (Thakkar

1956:47), any more than it is possible to ban racism, sexism, anti-Semitism, etc., by means of a decree in Western countries. Recognizing that Article 17 had been ineffective, the Parliament of India in 1955 passed the Anti-Untouchability (Offences) Act, which became effective 1 June 1955 (Sharma 1974:309). One provision tried to put teeth into the Constitutional Article 17 by saying that "imposition of social disabilities in respect of entry and worship at public temples, access to shops and restaurants . . . places of public resort and accommodation . . . has been made punishable with imprisonment which may extend to six months or fine which extend to five hundred rupees or both" (Sharma 1974:310).

The problem, as the reader might have guessed, was one of enforcement. Despite millions of reported violations of the 1955 Act, there were only a small handful of actual convictions. Most incidents of untouchability were never officially reported to the police (James and Reddy 1980:115). (For the classic discussion of this matter, see Galanter's "The Abolition of Disabilities—Untouchability and the Law" 1972 and Schermerhorn 1975.)

One difficulty in enforcing the Act of 1955 was that the term "untouchability" was never really defined anywhere in the Act's text (Sharma 1974:316). Nor for that matter was it defined in India's Constitution (James and Reddy 1980:114; Kamble 1982:150-151). Although the English term "untouchability" first appeared in print in 1909, it gained acceptance rather than clarity, according to Galanter (1972:243).

I suspect that the lack of precise definition of untouchability was not the real reason for the lack of enforcement of Article 17 of the Constitution and the 1955 Act of Parliament. The real reason almost certainly had to do with the fact that untouchability is an integral part of the caste system in India and, as such, cannot easily be dislodged from its long-established place in Indic culture. In any case, report after report complains that, despite the illegality of untouchability, it continues to persist, and these reports come from Indian, not Western, observers (Gandhi 1982-1983:272; Kshirsagar 1986:11; Sharma 1986:79; Rao 1989:119; Lal and Nahar 1990).

Some scholars have realized that untouchability is but one symptom of a larger problem. "There are ideologies behind the problem of untouchability which, in the name of religion and social justice, obstruct any attempt of a solution" (Fuchs 1950:435, n.141). More enlightening was the following view:

At the back of the monolithic concepts of untouchability was the idea of pure and impure or clean and unclean activities. As we have seen that in every district there are not more than two castes engaged in unclean activities and the unclean activities are not more than two namely, disposing and skinning the dead animals and sweeping the village. The latter activity in the rural areas is largely confined to the untouchable not so much because of its impurity as because of its very low evaluation in the secular hierarchy of occupations. (Desai 1976:166)

This raises the theoretical issue, perhaps partly chicken and egg, as to whether the low rank of the occupation *causes* the status of untouchability or whether their lowly status *requires* them to follow that occupation (cf. Hanumanthan 1979:54). One writer claims: "It is beside the point whether their low status in the society was due to the degrading nature of their occupations or they were condemned to follow these occupations because of their low status" (Khan 1980:82). It seems to me that this attitude begs the entire question of the ultimate meaning and significance of untouchability.

Most authorities simply throw up their hands in despair with respect to explaining the origin of untouchability. "No single phenomenon is enough to explain the origin of untouchability" (Parui 1961:4). "The origin of untouchability in India has been a puzzle and an enigma to all social historians. . . . It is too big a problem to be disposed of by one single explanation" (Hanumanthan 1979:29, 64).

One of the few attempts to offer an explanation suggested that untouchability "can be explained by the sibling rivalry concept. . . . The upper caste symbolizes the elder sibling and the lower caste the younger sibling" (Banerji 1980:131). While I would have no objection to invoking a principle of psychology to explain cultural behavior, it is not at all clear to me why sibling rivalry should be expressed specifically in terms of touching one another. Kubie, who mentions untouchables en passant in his classic essay, "The Fantasy of Dirt," considers them as an extreme example of labeling a strange or foreign group as "dirty." "It is as though man struggled to rid himself of his own secret inner uncleanliness by finding another and dirtier human being he could scorn" (Kubie 1937:403).

The standard "explanation" tends to be more descriptive than analytic. "Untouchable castes lie at the bottom of Indian society. Their lowness is ritually explained by their permanent impurity which derives from their association with death and organic pollution" (Deliège 1992:156). But why should an association with death and organic pollution result in *permanent* impurity? After all, high-caste members are able through various rituals to remove defilement caused by contact with an untouchable. Since the defiling acts by untouchables can be undone so to speak: "Should a well become polluted through being used by an Untouchable . . . purification can easily be arranged by pouring into it either a bucketful of Ganges water or drops of cow's urine from a small brass vessel" (Baker 1990:50), why is it that untouchables themselves cannot be 'purified' in some ritual way? Why is their defiling status *permanent*?

Untouchability continues to be a factor in India. While there is some indication that it may be declining in the public arena (Sinha 1960:169), e.g., with respect to public transport, postal service, and the public school system, it is still to be found in the private sector, e.g., inter-dining and temple entry (Gandhi 1982-1983:267; Misra 1982-1983; Sharma 1986:77). It also seems to be more common in rural as opposed to urban areas. In a study of untouchability in rural Gujarat, it was reported that "in more than 90 percent of villages temple entry and house entry are not permitted" (Desai 1976:263). Since 1955, untouchability has been against the law, but de jure is not de facto. It is my sincere hope that this attempt to explain the unconscious underlying folk belief complex, which has led to untouchability, may be of some help in bringing this strange and pernicious custom to an end.

## The First Tale of Crow and Sparrow

A considerable literature is devoted to the study of folktales in India (cf. Islam 1970; Upadhyaya, K. D. 1961; Upadhyaya, Hari S. 1968), but most of the emphasis has been on collection with minimal concern with analysis. Yet folktales, like all genres of folklore, represent folk models of the societies in which they are recounted. We may consider a folktale not only as a valuable mirror of the society to which its narrator and audience belong, but more importantly as a prime example of an "unobtrusive measure," so useful as a means of investigating that society. In contrast to the *a priori* questionnaires and projective tests brought to the field by supposedly objective social scientists, a folktale is a native construction, constructed without the inevitable bias of the outsider. If there is bias, it is at least the bias of the insider. The folktale that exists before the outsider even begins his or her investigation thus permits a native's view of his or her culture. This, in turn, has the potential of providing a unique window for the outsider who desires access to the innermost patterning of a given culture. This is why I choose to begin our intellectual odyssey in search of a plausible rationale or explanation for that aspect of caste known as "untouchability" with several folktales. It is my contention that the following two different folktales involving crow and sparrow will give the reader a critical clue about the nature of caste and untouchability in India.

The first tale of crow and sparrow is what folklorists term a cumulative tale, which is a subset of formula tales. A cumulative tale typically has a series of actions or events that may be either interrelated or not related. The brief summary of Aarne-Thompson tale type 2030B, Crow Must Wash His Bill In Order To Eat With Other Birds, says merely "Asks water; water must first have horn from stag, who must first have milk from cow, etc." (Aarne and Thompson 1961:529). A tale type summary hardly does justice to the full texts of the folktale in question. I shall present several versions of the tale so that the reader can come to appreciate the nuances and subtleties of the narrative.

One of the earliest modern versions, entitled "The Sparrow and the Crow," was reported in the *Indian Antiquary* in September 1880. Collected by Flora Annie Steel, it was accompanied by notes written by Lieutenant R. C. Temple. Here is that version with the Punjabi formula omitted:

A sparrow and a crow once agreed to cook *khijrî* [a dish of rice and dal] for their dinner. The crow brought pulse [mung] and the sparrow rice, and the sparrow cooked the *khijrî*. When it was ready, the crow came to claim his share. "No," said the sparrow, "you are dirty, go and wash your beak in the tank yonder, and after that, sit down to dinner."

So the crow went to the tank, and said,:

> You're Mr. Tank,
> I am Mr. Crow.
> Give me water
> That I may wash my beak,

And eat my *khijrî*.
See the bird's playfulness.
I am a clean crow.

But the tank said: "I will give you water if you will go to the deer, break off one of its horns, and dig a hole in the ground close by me, and then I'll let my water run in clean and fresh." So the crow said to the deer:

You are Mr. Deer,
I am Mr. Crow.
You give me a horn,
And I will dig a hole,
And take out the water,
That I may wash my beak,
And eat my *khijrî*.
See the bird's playfulness.
I am a clean crow.

But the deer said: "I'll give you my horn if you will give me some buffalo's milk, for then I shall grow fat, and breaking my horn won't hurt me." So the crow went to a buffalo and said:

You are Mrs. Buffalo,
I am Mr. Crow.
You give me milk,
That I may give it the deer to drink,
And break his horn,
And dig the hole,
And take out the water,
And wash my beak,
And eat my *khijrî*.
See the bird's playfulness.
I am a clean crow.

But the buffalo said: "Bring me some grass first, and I'll give you milk." So the crow went to some grass, and said:

You are Mr. Grass,
I am Mr. Crow.

> You give me some grass,
> That I may give it the buffalo,
> And take her milk,
> And give it the deer to drink,
> And break his horn,
> And dig the hole,
> And take out the water,
> And wash my beak,
> And eat my *khijrî*.
> See the bird's playfulness.
> I am a clean crow.

But the grass said: "Get a spade first, and then you can dig me up." So the crow went to a blacksmith, and said:

> You are Mr. Blacksmith,
> I am Mr. Crow.
> You give me a spade,
> And I will dig the grass,
> That I may give it the buffalo to eat,
> And take her milk,
> And give it the deer to drink,
> And break his horn,
> And dig the hole,
> And take out the water,
> And wash my beak,
> And eat my *khijrî*.
> See the bird's playfulness.
> I am a clean crow.

"With pleasure," said the blacksmith, "if you will light the fire and blow the bellows."

So the crow began to light the fire and blow the bellows, and in so doing fell into the middle of the fire and was burnt.

So that was the end of him, and the sparrow ate all the *khijrî*. (Steel and Temple, 1880:207-209). In a later version of this same tale by the same authors, published in 1894, we find considerable embroidery and elaboration (Steel, 1894:102-106), as was noted by the Czech folklorist Albert Wesselski in his brief comparison of the two versions

(1933:33-34) in the context of his criticism of the Finnish folklorist Martti Haavio's (1932:31-33) discussion of the tale. Haavio (not Paavio as cited by Emeneau 1943:272, n.2) was interested in the tale as an example of the cumulative folktale genre. Another allusion to the tale was made by the author of a general book on fairy tales who actually went so far as to recommend "The Sparrow and the Crow" as an ideal story to use in teaching English as a foreign language, presumably because of the built-in repetition of whole phrases (Kready 1916:125-126).

Sarat Chandra Mitra, the great Bengali folklorist and one of the most prolific folklorists who ever lived (Sengupta 1965: 53-87) presented a paper in 1901, in which he included a "hitherto unpublished" Bengali tale of "The Prawn and the Crow" (1903:102-103). In this tale a prawn is substituted for the more common sparrow. The crow wants to eat the prawn, but the latter escapes by saying, "Friend Crow, I have no objection to your eating me; but, as you eat all kinds of dirty things, I wish you would first wash your beak with water from the Ganges and then eat me." The Ganges demands an earthen cup, the potter demands a deer's horn (to dig the earth to make the cup), the deer demands grass, the grass-cutter demands a scythe, the blacksmith demands fire, and finally Fire "consented, but as the Crow went to take the fire, he was burnt and died."

More than twenty years later, Mitra (1927) again discussed this formula tale. His analytic comments are limited to the suggestion that digging earth with a deer horn indicates a Neolithic allusion insofar as iron implements were presumably not yet available (1927:11) and the further hypothesis that since the blacksmith asks for fire (instead of kindling it himself), this may be a reference to "some long-standing taboo—some primitive prohibition, *which forbade him to kindle a fire*" (1927:16). Possibly more germane is the ritual use of a deer's horn in connection with Brahmanic urination. According to the *Satapatha-Brahmana* (Eggeling 1885:43): "When he intends to pass urine, he takes up a clod of earth . . . by means of the deer's horn . . ." He then urinates on the uncovered area of earth after which he returns the clod to its original place. Having lifted up the earth's covering, "he has relieved himself on its impure body, and now restores to it this its covering" (Eggeling 1885:44).

Another Bengali version, this time from Bangladesh (Jasmuddin 1967:35-40), has the more common crow and sparrow characters. In this tale, entitled "The Poor Crow," the sparrow refuses to be friends with the crow, saying "You are a crow and you are dirty. Please go away." Sparrow finally agrees to be friends on condition that the crow go wash his beak in the river. The series of potential donors ends with a farmer who brings an iron bowl full of fire, but when the crow flapped his wings, it fanned the flames and "the flames burned the crow's feathers." "So the poor crow died without ever having the sparrow as his friend."

In another version from Bangladesh, "The Crow and the Sparrow" (Siddiqui 1980:23-34), Crow and Sparrow have a contest eating red peppers—the winner to eat the loser. Crow wins, but Sparrow demands, "If you want my meat, you must wash your beak." Again the series of donors is recited ending with the farmer's wife to whom the Crow says:

> Dear farmer's wife! Give me fire.
> I will take the fire to the blacksmith,
> who will make me a spade.
> I will take the spade and dig some clay,
> Take the clay and give it to the
> pottery maker to make a pot.
> I will take the pot,
> Go to the river, wash my beak,
> Make myself neat,
> And eat the sweet sparrow's meat.

The farmer's wife put the fire upon the back of the crow, and the greedy crow was "burnt to ashes" (Siddiqui 1980:34).

In still another Bengali version of the tale, reported by the grandfather of film director Satyajit Ray (Raychaudhuri 1981:33-36), we find the same chili-eating contest with the winner crow earning the right to peck out sparrow's heart. In the final episode, a householder puts embers on the crow's wings "and the silly creature was burnt to death."

In a final Bengali version reported by the late Sankar Sengupta more than one hundred years later than the first one cited above, we find that sparrow was eating paddy and the crow was eating pepper. The crow proposed, "Whoever of us will finish eating all the grains of the field will be the winner and the winner will eat a bit of meat from the chest of the other" as the winner's prize. The sparrow doubted that the crow could eat all the pepper in the field, but the crow hid ten peppers for every one that he ate. Winning the contest, crow claimed his prize, but sparrow said, "Dear crow, I have a little request to make of you. You go to different places and eat different dirty and filthy articles. So you will have to wash your lips before you enter on my breast for eating my meat." Crow assents, but at the river, the river speaks, "Hallow crow, you consume different dirty and filthy articles through your lips. If you dip your lips in the water, all the water of the river will be spoiled. So better bring a small jar and carry water for washing your lips." Crow then goes to a potter who asks crow to bring clay. The clay said, "Crow, your lips are dirty—you cannot dig mud with your lips. If you want clay, bring a small spade for digging mud." At the blacksmith to obtain a spade, the blacksmith asks for fire. Looking for fire, the crow meets a dog who advises crow to go back to the blacksmith to get a sickle, give a sickle to the shepherd to cut grass, give the grass to cows who will give milk, bring the milk to the dog, who strengthened, will kill a buffalo. "By the horn of that buffalo you will dig the mud and carry that mud to the potter for making a water-vessel." The crow liked the advice and went to a nearby household and said:

> Oh the master of the house, please give me a little fire.
> The black-smith will manufacture a sickle,
> Your cow-boy will cut the grass by that,
> The grass will be devoured by your cows.
> As a result they will give fresh and extra milk.
> The extra milk will again be drunk by the dog.
> By which the dog will be so strengthened
> That it will be able to kill a buffalo.
> I will take the horn of the dead buffalo and will dig the mud.
> Then I will carry clay to the potter for making a water-pot.
> I will carry water in the pot and will wash my lips.
> I too will be able to split the breast.
> I too will be able to split the breast of the sparrow.
> So will be able to eat its meat."

The master of the house is willing to give the crow some fire and asks crow where to put it. "'Please put the fire on my back.' But as soon as the master of the house placed fire on the back of the crow, it burnt the crow to ashes" (Sengupta 1991:193-195).

These versions of the tale are representative. There are also plenty of non-Bengali versions of the tale: "The Crow and the Sparrow"

(Anon 1892:138); "The Old Woman and the Crow" (Anon 1895:142); "The Crow and the Sparrow" (Elwin 1944:473-475); "The Raven and the Wren" (Borooah 1955:17-22); "The Crow and the Bitter Gourd (Das and Mahapatra 1979:138-141); and "The Crow and the Wren" (Goswami 1980: 215-218).

Burma, which, of course, is contiguous to India, also has a version of the folktale. Again, it is a wren rather than a sparrow who is opposed to the crow antagonist. The Crow asks the Wren's father for permission to eat the Wren. "You eat all sort of rubbish," said the Wren, "and your beak is dirty. My daughter is clean and sweet, and unless you wash your mouth in front of me, I cannot put my daughter in your beak." Crow visits the usual series of intermediaries, ending with a visit to Fire: "Fire, Fire, come with me, To burn the Forest, To clear the Land, To grow the Grass, To feed the Buffalo, To wallow the Mud, To mend the Pot, To fetch the Water, To wash the Beak, To eat the little Wren." Crow flies back toward the Forest with Fire in his beak, but his beak becomes so badly burned that he had to drop Fire and give up all hope of eating little Wren (Aung 1952:21-25). (For a version from Nepal, see Sakya and Griffith 1980:222-224.)

Despite the variety in dramatis personae, the basic structure of the tale seems fairly consistent. Occasionally, the characters of crow and sparrow have their roles reversed. In these, it is the sparrow rather than the crow who is punished in the end. Consider the following Punjabi variant of the tale. (This Punjabi version was collected from Baijit Dhillon Vikram Singh in Los Altos Hills in 1988 by her daughter who was a student in my folklore class. Her mother learned the tale in the Punjab in India, circa 1946.)

*Once upon a time, there was a crow and a sparrow. They got together and decided they were going to make khitcherie, rice and lentils (gruel). The sparrow said to the crow, "Crow, crow, run and find the rice." The crow said, "I will, You go get the lentils." Both of them flew their own way and came back after a while, the crow with the rice, the sparrow with the lentils. However, the crow brought the rice back slowly, one kernel at a time, that the farmers had left in the fields while the sparrow quickly brought back lentils after stealing them from an old lady (or cripple). They both got together and cooked a wonderful khitcherie.*

*Then the sparrow looked at the crow and said, "Crow, you have a dirty beak. You need to bathe yourself and come back and then we'll eat our khitcherie." The crow looks at himself and said, "Yes, I need to clean up," and he flew away to have a bath in the pond singing, "I'm going to come back from the pond clean with red socks around my feet ("tum tum karke eye-ya. . . .")*

*Meanwhile, the sparrow ate up all the khitcherie, put the lid on the pot and hid in the room. The crow came back and lifted the lid and found nothing in the pot. He was so mad that he looked around and found a long needle. He stuck it into the fire and got it red hot and said, "Sparrow, sparrow—come, I have a present for you." Sparrow came slowly out of hiding. Crow stuck it in her tail. And Sparrow said, "Choo, choo, my tail is burning." Crow said, "Right, ho, why did you eat my share of the khitcherie?"*

It is noteworthy in this case that the informant indicated that the ending varied depending upon the make-up of the audience. If the story is told to children, sparrow hides in the stove, and crow turns on the stove as punishment, thereby burning sparrow. If the story is told to adults, then the needle is stuck up the rear end of the sparrow.

I shall defer analysis of this tale until after presenting the second tale of crow and sparrow, but there is one analytic issue I should like to settle here and now. The question is: are we or are we not justified in interpreting this cumulative tale of "The Sparrow and the Crow" as an allegory or parable about the caste system and untouchability? To answer this important question, consider one last version of the tale, this one reported from Maharashtra in West Central India in 1959 (Bhagvat 1959:215):

*There was a crow who wanted to eat a sparrow's nestlings. He once went to her house and asked for the desired feast. The sparrow was shrewd and knew that she was unable to give an open fight to her stronger opponent. She thought for a while and said meekly to the crow, "Oh crow! You can surely eat my babies if you want. But there is one condition. You know that you are a Mahar, an untouchable, and I am a Brahman, so please do not touch my babies as you are. You must wash yourself, beak and all, and then eat them up."*

*"So be it," said the crow and went to the river. As he was about to take a dip in the water, the river said, "Oh, crow, you are a Mahar, so do not enter my water."*

*"Oh river, I have to bathe in the water and then go and eat the*

*sparrow's nestlings."*

　　*"In that case, bring a pot and take water in it."*

　　*The crow then went to a potter and said, "Oh potter, give me a pot. With the pot I bring water. With the water I bathe. After bathing I eat the sparrow's nestlings."*

　　*"In that case," said the potter, "you have to get me earth; because all the pots that are here are broken."*

　　*The crow then went to the earth and started digging the earth with his beak and he was not able to do much digging. So he went to the deer and begged for its horn. The deer said that, if the crow could arrange a fight with a dog, then only its horn would be broken. The crow went to a dog and begged him to fight with the deer and thus help him with the horn, so that he could dig the earth and thus get a pot made by the potter and then having washed his mouth, he could feast on sparrow's nestlings. The dog consented to fight but said, "Oh crow! I need an iron ball to throw at the deer. So get it for me." The crow then went to the ironsmith and begged for the ball. The smith made a ball in the fire and gave it to the crow. The crow held the hot burning ball in his beak and was burnt to death. The sparrow was thus spared her young ones.*

Here we see clearly that the contrast between the clean sparrow Brahman and dirty crow Mahar is explicit with respect to caste and untouchability. We shall now proceed to the second tale involving crow and sparrow.

## The Second Tale of Crow and Sparrow

In this tale, a crow seeks shelter with sparrow, usually after a rainstorm has destroyed crow's abode. With some reluctance, sparrow finally admits crow to her home, but crow repays the sparrow's kindness either by eating sparrow's food supply (Bødker tale type 1046) or by eating sparrow's young ones (Bødker tale type 918). The latter form of the tale is almost certainly a cognate of Asian (Chinese, Japanese, Korean) versions of Aarne-Thompson tale type 123, The Wolf and the Kids, which in turn is genetically related to Aarne-Thompson tale type 333, The Glutton (Red Riding Hood) (cf. Dundes 1989:200-203). I shall demonstrate this Indic tale's relationship to Little Red Riding Hood later in this essay. In any event, the tale is well known throughout India and is especially popular with very young children. Novelist Shashi Deshpande in her 1988 *That Long Silence* referred to the tale as one "which we were told as soon as we got into the 'tell me a story' phase. It was the first story told to us, the first I can remember, the first perhaps told to all children" (1988:16). This sentiment is echoed by Indumati Sheorey when she remarked that it is "perhaps the first story that the Maharashtrian mother tells her child" (Sheorey 1973:11).

I shall present a number of different versions of the tale so that the reader can become familiar with its various manifestations, following the same procedure as with the first tale of Crow and Sparrow. Partly for sentimental reasons, I shall begin with Professor A. K. Ramanujan's Kannada version:

*Sister Crow and Sister Sparrow are friends. Crow has a house of cowdung; Sparrow, one of stone. A big rainstorm washes away Crow's house. So she comes to Sparrow and knocks on her door. Sparrow makes her wait—first because she is feeding her children, later because she is making her husband's and children's bed. Finally she lets her in and offers her several places to sleep. Crow chooses to sleep in the chickpea sacks. All night she munches chickpea and makes a katum-katum noise. Whenever Sparrow asks her what the noise is, Crow says, "Nothing really. Remember, you gave me a betel-nut? I'm biting on it." By morning, she has eaten up all the chickpeas in the sack. She cannot control her bowels, so she fills the sack with her shit before she leaves. Sparrow's children go in the morning to eat some peas, and muck their hands up with Crow's shit.*

*Sparrow is angry. When Crow comes back that night to sleep, she [Sparrow] puts a hot iron spatula under her [Crow] and brands her behind. Crow flees, crying Kä! Kä! in pain.* (Ramanujan 1987:121; cf. 1989:256; 1997:161-163)

One might ask just how old is this tale? We can easily trace it back one hundred years for we have an abridged version reported from Bhopal in 1896. In this fragmentary version, we have a sparrow who comes to borrow some salt to season her curry and rice from a crow who was building her nest of salt. The crow refuses. When the rains come, crow's salt nest dissolved, and she went to sparrow asking, "Let me have a place in your dry nest." But sparrow replied, "When I wanted some salt, you had none to give me, and now you want a dry spot and I have none to give you" (Taylor 1896:88). But it turns out that the tale is older than 1896. Perhaps the first version of the tale to appear in English was the Lingaet text recorded by Mary Frere in her *Old Deccan Days*, published in 1868. The daughter of a popular administrator, Sir Bartle Frere, the governor of the Bombay Presidency, Frere collected twenty-four tales from her nursemaid-governess, Anna Liberata de Souza, during the winter of 1865-1866. (Her father wrote the introduction and notes to the volume. For details about Mary Frere, see Islam 1970:177-186.) Frere's text is somewhat unusual insofar as two crows, rather than one, seeks sanctuary with a sparrow. Still, it is apparently the female crow that does the talking for herself and "her mate."

## The Selfish Sparrow and the Houseless Crows

*A sparrow once built a nice little house for herself, and lined it well with wood, and protected it with sticks, so that it equally resisted the summer sun and the winter rains. A Crow, who lived close by, had also built a house, but it was not such a good one, being only made of a few sticks laid one above another on the top of a prickly pear hedge. The consequence was that, one day when there was an unusually heavy shower, the Crow's nest was washed away, while the Sparrow's was not at all injured.*

*In this extremity the Crow and her mate went to the Sparrow, and said, "Sparrow, Sparrow, have pity on us, and give us shelter, for the wind blows, and the rain beats, and the prickly pear hedge thorns stick into our eyes." But the Sparrow answered, "I'm cooking the dinner, I cannot let you in now, come again presently." In a little while the Crows returned, and said, "Sparrow, Sparrow, have pity on us, and give us shelter, for the wind blows, and the rain beats, and the prickly pear hedge thorns stick into our eyes." The Sparrow answered, "I'm eating my dinner, I cannot let you in now, come again presently." The Crows flew away, but in a little while returned, and cried once more, "Sparrow, Sparrow, have pity on us, and give us shelter, for the wind blows, and the rain beats, and the prickly pear hedge thorns stick into our eyes." The Sparrow replied, "I'm washing the dishes, I cannot let you in now, come again presently." The Crows waited a while and then called out,*

*"Sparrow, Sparrow, have pity on us, and give us shelter, for the wind blows, and the rain beats, and the prickly pear hedge thorns stick into our eyes." But the Sparrow would not let them in, she only answered, "I'm sweeping the floor, I cannot let you in now, come again presently." Next time the Crows came and cried, "Sparrow, Sparrow, have pity on us, and give us shelter, for the wind blows, and the rain beats, and the prickly pear hedge thorns stick into our eyes"—she answered, "I'm making the beds, I cannot let you in now, come again presently." So, on one pretence or another, she refused to help the poor birds. At last, when she and her children had their dinner, and she had prepared and put away the dinner for next day, and had put all the children to bed and gone to bed herself, she cried to the Crows, "You may come in now, and take shelter for the night." The Crows came in, but they were very vexed at having been kept out so long in the wind and the rain, and when the Sparrow and all her family were asleep, the one said to the other, "This selfish Sparrow had no pity on us, she gave us no dinner, and would not let us in, till she and all her children were comfortably in bed; let us punish her." So the two Crows took all the nice dinner the Sparrow had prepared for herself and her children to eat next day, and flew away with it.* (Frere 1868:139-140)

This 1865 version certainly differs from the Kannada text cited above. The hearer's sympathy tends to be with the homeless crows who are forced to wait to come in out of the rain and wind by an apparently heartless and callous sparrow. It is tempting to speculate that the context—that is, a servant telling a tale to her young mistress—might explain why the "rich" sparrow is implicitly criticized and no blame attached to the two crows taking "all the nice dinner the Sparrow had prepared for herself and her children." The nursemaid who is presumably living in the mistress's home could easily identify with the crows. In any event, the lesson for students of folklore is that it would be a serious mistake to analyze this folktale on the basis of a single version, especially if that version were Frere's. Her version contains nary a hint of any anal theme.

We have not yet concluded our attempt to find earlier versions of our tale. There is good evidence that the tale is much, much older than 1865.

In *Lilacaritra*, the biography of the thirteenth-century founder of the Mahanubhava sect of Hinduism, Chakradhar, we find a version of the story attributed to this saint who used it to instruct one of his female disciples. The woman insisted upon applying the same facial paste used by the Swami to give him a fair (white) complexion. No one could dissuade her so the saint allegedly took on the form of a child and called out to the woman to listen to a story: "The crow's house was built out of cow dung. The sparrow's house was built out of wax. There was a big rainstorm and the crow's house was destroyed. The sparrow's house was still standing. [Crow comes seeking shelter with Sparrow.] The sparrow replies angrily from within her house, 'Crow, Crow I cannot see you or hear you now.' Sparrow repeats this three times. Listening to this story, the female disciple is appeased and gives up her demand to use the Swami's facial paste" (1982:108). Presumably the point of this archaic Marathi version of the tale is that black cannot become white. In any event, as brief as this version is, it does provide a useful *terminus ante quem* for the tale indicating that it is more than eight hundred years old.

It should be obvious that both the nineteenth-century versions and the thirteenth-century Marathi version of the story omit most of the folktale's content, but such censorship is perfectly understandable in context. Most pre-twentieth-century collections of folktales—all over the world—were censored. India was no exception. Let us now consider a Tamil version of our tale:

## A Crow and a Sparrow

*In a village, a crow and a sparrow had lived as friends. They said that they needed a house to stay in during the rainy season and added that they would build a house. After consultation, both thought of building a house. With much difficulty, the sparrow built a house made of stones, but the crow built a house made of sand. Though the sparrow tried to persuade the crow not to build a house made of sand, the crow turned a deaf ear. Both of them lived in their respective houses happily.*

*The rainy season came. The crow's house got dissolved in rain water. But the sparrow's house did not dissolve. The crow knocked at the door of the sparrow's house. The sparrow said, "I am preparing eatables for my children." After some time, the crow said, "Sparrow, Sparrow, please open the door!" The sparrow opened the door and asked the crow to stay on the third floor. There the sparrow kept the eatables in various vessels for its nestlings. After having eaten all the eatables, the crow filled the vessels up with its excreta. The nestlings of the sparrow, after having played, came home and asked, "Mummy, we are hungry. Give us some eatables." Mummy said, "I have kept them on the third floor. Take them and eat." The nestlings with all desire, went upstairs and placed their hands into the vessels. Their hands became full of excreta. Immediately they went to their mother and told her that the crow, after having eaten all the eatables in the vessels, filled them up with its excreta. At that time, the crow had gone out to wander. The sparrow with all anger, telling "You ate what I kept for my children," waited after having filled a big vessel with hot water. As soon as the crow came, the sparrow said, "I have got hot water for you. You need not bathe in cold water in the rainy season. You jump into hot water and bathe." With all desire, the crow jumped into the hot water to take a bath. It got itself burned and died. Immediately, the sparrow threw away the crow, and it lived with its children happily.* [This tale was collected by A. Sivasubramanian from a 19-year-old zoology student on 20 September 1990 in Tuticorin.]

Next is a Telugu version of the tale.

## The Crow and the Sparrow

*Once upon a time, there lived a crow and a sparrow in a village. Crow's house was built by small twigs, and the sparrow has a strong building. One day all of a sudden a big storm with heavy wind and rain came. The house of the crow was dismantled because it was constructed of small twigs. Then the crow went to the sparrow's house to seek shelter and knocked at the door. The answer from the sparrow was, "Wait a minute. I am bathing my boy." After a minute, the crow once again knocked at the door. The answer was, "Wait a minute. My boy is going to bed." After some time, the crow knocked at the door again. Then the sparrow told, "Wait a minute. I am bathing my husband." After some time, the crow did the same, and sparrow answered, "I am giving food to my husband." Then the crow once again knocked at the door. The sparrow replied in the same manner, "Wait a minute, my husband is going to bed."*

*After some time, the sparrow opens the door and invites the crow into the house. The crow explained all what happened to her house and asked the sparrow for a place to sleep. Then the sparrow with pity showing a room, questioned the crow, "Where will you sleep? On the dry coconut-kernel barrel or the betel-nut barrel?" Then the crow immediately tells that she will sleep on the dry coconut-kernel barrel. The sparrow accepted this and told the crow to sleep "where you like," and she went to her bed. At midnight the crow started eating the dry coconut kernels. The sparrow heard and asked the crow what the sound is. The crow answered that the foolish merchant had given her unripened betel nut. "I am trying to cut it with difficulty." The sparrow asked, "Can I do it for you?" "No, no! I ate it." In that way the crow ate all of the dry coconut kernel and left excretion filling up the barrel. Early in the morning when sparrow opened the door, the crow left calmly.*

*When the sparrow's boy wanted a dry coconut before going to school, the sparrow took the boy to the barrel and made the boy get in the barrel to get the dry coconut kernel. The boy dipped into the excretion and cried. Then the sparrow came to know the crow's mischief, and sparrow got angry. Then the sparrow took an iron rod and heated it until it was red hot. In the evening, as soon as the crow entered the house, the sparrow closed all the windows and doors and took the red hot iron rod and forcibly stuck it into the anal cavity of the crow. Then the crow cried and tried to escape, going all around the house. The sparrow, thinking that the crow had gotten good enough punishment, opened the door. As soon as the door was opened, the crow with cries flew out of the house.* [This tale was collected in 1988 by V. Subrahmanyam, a 38-year-old lecturer in Lexicography at Telugu University from himself. He had heard it as a child in the late 1950s in a small village, Chiyyapad, in the Cuddapah district of Andhra Pradesh.]

The following text is an Urdu version of the tale.

## The Crow and the Sparrow

*Once there lived a crow and a sparrow. Both of them were good friends. The crow's house was made of salt, and the sparrow's house was made of wax. One night it started raining heavily, and the crow's house, which was made of salt, got dissolved. The crow got scared and quickly approached sparrow's house seeking shelter. On reaching the sparrow's house, she knocked at the door, but sparrow did not open it quickly. After enquiring who it was, the sparrow informed the crow from inside that she was busy with her domestic chores and asked the crow to wait for a while. By that time, the crow, waiting outside, got completely drenched in rain.*

*After some time, the sparrow opened the door and allowed the crow to come inside the house. The crow requested the sparrow to give her some place in a corner of the house for a night so that she could rest and sleep. The sparrow hesitated for a while, and then asked the crow whether it would rather sleep on a sack containing Bengal grain or on a sack containing peanuts. The crow who was hungry and wanted to enjoy eating peanuts, said slowly that she would not mind sleeping on a rough sack of peanuts. When everyone slept, the crow started eating peanuts. The sparrow heard the noise of (munching sound) munching and she asked the crow what it was doing. The crow answered that she was eating the betel nuts given to her by her mother-in-law. In this way the crow spent the whole night eating all the peanuts in the sack and filling it instead with its shit. When it stopped raining in the morning, the crow thanked the sparrow and flew away. When sparrow came to pick peanuts from the sack to feed its kids, the sack was full of shit and sparrow got very angry. The sparrow decided to teach a lesson to the crow. After a few days, the sparrow invited the crow for a feast. The sparrow told the crow to wash her hands and face and as the crow started to wash, the sparrow along with its friends poured boiling water over the crow. She screamed and flew away.* (This Urdu version was collected by Zubeeda Banu in 1988 from herself. She had learned the tale from her grandmother in Madras in 1968.]

Thus far versions of our second tale involve the crow's devouring the sparrow's food supply. In the other popular form of the tale, the crow eats the sparrow's young. It should perhaps be noted that there is a folk tradition of crows eating the young of other birds. For example, a Coorg finger rhyme-song (Rao 1925-1926:33) entitled "Doves Family," goes as follows:

> Cooing, cooing, cooing dove!
> How many young ones have you?
> Five little ones I have hatched.
> Where are the little ones now?
> On a strong bough I left them.
> I cannot see them on the bough,
> A crow has carried them off.

Two Kannada versions of this form of the tale should suffice.

## The Sparrow and the Crow

*Once upon a time, there lived a crow and a sparrow. The crow's hut was made of straw but the sparrow's was built of stone. One day the birds went in search of food. On that day there was a heavy rain and the crow's house was washed away. When the crow returned in the late evening, there was no house.*

*The crow remembered her friend the sparrow and arrived at her house. The door was closed.*

*"Sister Sparrow, Sister Sparrow, will you open the door for me?" said the crow.*

*"I am bathing my young baby," said the sparrow from inside.*

*"Sister Sparrow, Sister Sparrow, will you open the door? It is too chill outside," said the crow again.*

*"I am feeding the baby," said the sparrow from inside.*

*"Sister Sparrow, Sister Sparrow, will you open the door for me?" requested the crow very humbly.*

*"I am putting my baby to sleep," said the sparrow.*

*When the crow requested again, the sparrow opened the door.*

*"Sister Sparrow, Sister Sparrow, my hut was washed away in the rain. Will you give me a room to sleep today?" asked the crow. The sparrow agreed, but asked, "Where will you sleep? Will you rest in my cowshed?"*

*"No, no. I may be trampled to death by the cow."*

*"Will you sleep by the wall?" asked the sparrow.*

*"No, no. The wall may fall on me."*

*"Will you sleep under the cradle?" once again asked the sparrow.*

*"No, no. What if the cradle falls down upon me?"*

*"Then will you sleep in the cradle?"*

*The crow readily agreed and slept inside the cradle with the sparrow's young ones. The sparrow also slept near the cradle. At midnight, a sound, "kutum," was heard. The sparrow asked the crow, "What are you eating?"*

*"Yesterday, I went to Kōta and bought a piece of copra [dry coconut] and I ate it," said the crow.*

*After a short while, again another sound, "kutum," was heard.*

*Again the sparrow asked the crow, "What is it?"*

*"Yesterday I went to Kundapur shandy and bought an areca nut. I ate it."*

*After a short while, again the sound, "kutum," was heard, and again the sparrow questioned the crow.*

*"Yesterday I purchased a ground nut at Kōteswar festival, and ate it now."*

*Early in the morning the crow went out and flew away. The sparrow went up to the cradle to feed her younger ones. But, alas, there was not a single baby! It realised the trick by the crow.*

*"Wait, I will teach a lesson to the deceitful crow," said the sparrow.*

*It bought some lime, boiled it, and made a paste. Putting the paste on a plate, sparrow went round asking, "Who wants butter?" The crow ate the hot lime and at once its stomach burst out. All the baby sparrows came out alive. The mother sparrow washed them and carried them away.* [This Kannada tale was collected on July 22, 1988, in Kundapur by A. Navada, reader in Kannada at Bhandarkari College, from a 32-year-old Brahman woman who had learned the tale twenty-five years previously from her grandmother.]

Our last full text of the tale is also from Kannada tradition:

## The Story of Crow and Sparrow

*Once there lived a crow and a sparrow. The house of crow was made of cowdung and that of sparrow of mud. The crow was very cunning by its nature, but the sparrow was very gentle. Anyway, both were friends.*

*After a few months, the sparrow was pregnant and she had some babies in due course. The crow came to know this news immediately. She was tempted to eat the babies and planned to visit the sparrow's house. One day the crow went to the house of sparrow and knocked at the door. It was raining heavily. Hearing the noise in the late night, the sparrow asked, "Who is that?" The crow replied, "It is crow, your friend," and asked, "Please open the door!"*

*The sparrow then opened the door and asked the crow, "Why did you come in this late night?" The crow told, "Don't you know that my house is made of cowdung? Due to this heavy rain, it has been washed away into water. What can I do? I cannot stand in this piercing cold. Please give me a little place to sleep in this night."*

*The sparrow was very sad to hear the tale of the crow. It was kind enough to provide accommodation inside its house. It suggested that the crow sleep near the door, but the crow did not want to sleep near the door. So the crow said, "Should I sleep near the door? If it falls down due to the storm, definitely I will die. No, no! I won't sleep there." The sparrow then asked the crow to sleep near the wall. But the crow said, "Should I sleep there? If it falls down due to the heavy rain, I will be buried inside! No, no! I won't sleep near the wall at all!"*

*At last the sparrow showed the cradle and said, "See my babies are sleeping in the cradle. If you want, you can sleep there." The crow was very happy now. It also preferred the same place. At once it flew and jumped inside the cradle and slept near the babies of the sparrow.*

*In the middle of the night when the babies fell sleep, the crow picked up one baby and swallowed it. But when it swallowed, the sparrow heard the sound, "kutum." She asked the crow, "What is that sound, 'kutum,' 'kutum'?" The crow replied, "It is nothing, but I am eating the grain which I brought from my home to avoid the cold."*

*The sparrow did not worry about it and kept quiet by saying, "Oh, is it so?" It slept herself. After a little time, the crow caught another baby and swallowed it. The sparrow once again heard the sound, "kutum," "kutum." She asked, "Crow, crow, what is that 'kutum' 'kutum'?" The crow said, "It is nothing but I am eating the same grain, 'kutum' 'kutum.'" The sparrow kept quiet after saying, "Oh, is it so?" and slept without worrying about it.*

*But the crow swallowed all the babies and went away in the dark. In the morning when the sparrow peeped inside the cradle, its babies were not there. It was very sad. At the same time, it was very angry also. So it decided to teach a lesson to the crow.*

*When it was night, the crow came once again in the next day. The sparrow welcomed the crow and gave her something to eat. Then she called the crow to come near the oven to sit in front of the fire for warming up from the chilliness. When the crow sat down near the oven, the sparrow asked, "Crow, crow, open your mouth. I shall give you some freshly prepared sweets." The crow opened its mouth with great temptation. The sparrow at once threw a stone into the mouth of the crow—the stone was heated into red hot. The crow swallowed it without knowing anything about it. Immediately, crow's stomach began to burn with pain. As a result, it vomited everything outside. When it vomited, all the babies of the sparrow ran to the mother crying, "Chimu, chimu." The sparrow was extremely happy to see its babies alive. It at once embraced them. The crow learned a good lesson without staying a moment, disappeared with burning pain, and it never went back to the sparrow's house again.* [This tale was collected by Vamana Nandarara from a 70-year-old female informant from Jeppu, Mangalore, on February 6, 1987.]

There are other versions of this second tale available. For example, Emeneau reported (1946:207-215) an interesting Kota variant, entitled "The Sparrow and the Crow." A crow unable to withstand the rain and wind comes to sparrow's dwelling seeking shelter. Sparrow offers crow a place on the veranda, a place near the rubbish hole near the door, a place in the kitchen, and a place on the drying rack, all of which are refused in turn by crow. Finally crow asks to sleep in the attic, a request reluctantly granted by sparrow. In the attic, crow proceeds to eat meat, puffed grain, fruit, milk, plus the eggs and the young ones of the sparrow. While eating, the crow smacked its lips making a noise, "mack," "mack." When questioned about the noise by sparrow, crow replied that it was the noise made by its wet wings flapping. Later a friendly grandmother comes to lecture the sparrow on having been too nice to "that crow excrement-mouth," admonishing her, "Hereafter you must not join with yourself those evil ones."

The key telltale motif in this second crow and sparrow story is the strange noise made by the crow intruder during the night, a noise that the crow attempts to explain away when interrogated by the suspicious sparrow. This motif clearly links the tale of crow and sparrow with Aarne-Thompson tale type 123, "The Wolf and the Kids." The motif in question appears to be motif G87, "Cannibal crunching human bone says noise is only eating of peas." In the Chinese, Japanese, and Korean versions of Aarne-Thompson tale type 123/333, an ogress in disguise, typically as a tigress, gains access to her victim's house. Upon entering, she sleeps in the same bed as children-victims, and during the night begins eating them one by one. When one of the girls, the heroine, hears a strange munching sound, the tigress attempts to allay her suspicion by claiming that she is eating a peanut, bean or melon seed (Eberhard 1989:40-41). This is a very close parallel to the incident in the tale of Crow and Sparrow. However, in the Chinese and Japanese tales, the alert child asks for a sample of the food being consumed and when she is given her baby sibling's finger, she realizes her danger. (cf. Ting 1978:61 [type 333C The Tiger Grandma]; Ikeda 1971:92 [type 333A The Gluttonous Ogress and Children]). This detail is not found in Indic tales of Crow and Sparrow. Still, there can be no real question of the genetic relationship of Crow and Sparrow (second tale) to Little Red Riding Hood (AT 333). Any reader who takes the time to compare the versions of Crow and Sparrow in this essay with the 241 versions surveyed by Wolfram Eberhard (1989) can verify this. Even the element in one of the Kannada versions that has the sparrow dupe the crow into swallowing hot lime paste is strikingly similar to a Chinese version in which the heroine "pours lime, salt water, or hot liquid on her [the ogress's] body or into her mouth" (Ting 1978:62).

In a version of the tale from Kerala collected in 1979 entitled "The Crane and the Crow" (Beck et al. 1987:194-196), the crane takes revenge by covering a stone with cooked rice and placing the resulting rice ball on her roof. The crow "swallowed the ball greedily and the stone as well." The bird becomes dizzy, falls off the roof, its eyes pop out, and it dies of pain. The swallowing-of-the-stone "punishment" is strangely reminiscent of the Grimm tales, "The Wolf and the Seven Young Kids" (AT 123) and "Little Red Cap," insofar as the wolves in both those tales are punished by having stones inserted in their stomachs. Yet another clue pointing to the cognation of the tale to AT 123/333 is the presence of Motif F 913, Victims rescued from swallower's belly, in both the Indic and European tales. In one children's book version, sparrow shoves red-hot tongs down Crow's throat. "Out burst her little ones from inside, and they all lived happily ever after" (Spellman 1967:14).

The identification of our second tale of Crow and Sparrow with Little Red Riding Hood is probably of more interest to folklorists than to Indologists, but ultimately the identification will enhance our understanding of Little Red Riding Hood. For instance, we note that nearly all of our versions of Crow and Sparrow (second tale) were told by women. It is very much a woman-centered tale with female protagonists. Novelist Deshpande recognized this intuitively when she offers the following comment on our second tale:

> I have a feeling that even if little boys can forget the story,
> little girls never will. They will store this story in their

subconscious, their unconscious or whatever, and eventually
they will become that damnably, insufferably priggish sparrow
looking after their homes, their babies . . . and to hell with
the rest of the world. (Despande 1988:17)

The female-centeredness of the tale conforms to the other Asian
versions of the tale type. What this suggests is that the "wolf" of
European versions of the tale was probably a late addition or substitution
of a male villain in a place of an original female villain. As a general
rule, there is same-sex opposition in fairy tales, e.g., heroines facing
witches or evil stepmothers, and heroes contending with giants or
dragons. So it makes sense to argue that the original form of Little Red
Riding Hood, as found in many Asian versions of the tale type,
presumably had a girl heroine outwitting a female opponent. But all this
is beside the point with respect to our principal objective, namely, to
explicate the underlying psychological rationale of caste and
untouchability. So let us now turn to some analysis of our two distinct
folktales.

## Analysis of the Tales

In order to analyze the two folktales, we must begin by
explaining the concept of *oicotype*, a key theoretical notion in
contemporary folkloristics. Coined by Swedish folklorist C. W. von
Sydow (father of famed actor Max von Sydow) in 1927 (Bødker 1965:
220), the concept refers to a "special version of a folktale, developed by
isolation in a certain cultural area, by which on account of special
national, political, and geographical conditions, it takes a form different
from that of the same tale in other areas." The very definition of
oicotypes implies the utilization of the comparative method. Without a
comparative approach, one cannot possibly know what characteristics, if
any, of a particular folktale are peculiar to a local cultural environment.
The determination of an oicotype or oicotypical features is critical with
respect to undertaking studies of national, regional, or local character.
If a given feature is found in many versions of a folktale distributed in
many different cultures, it would be folly to claim that the specific
feature is unique to just one culture. Yet this is precisely what culturally
relativistic anthropologists are wont to do in studying the folklore of

"their" people, "their" village, without ever bothering to check to see if neighboring peoples and villages have exactly the same folktale or feature. (For further discussion of oicotypes, see Honko 1980 and Cochrane 1987; for oicotypes in India, see Beck 1987 and Ramanujan 1983.)

We have potential oicotypical details in both of our crow and sparrow folktales. For one thing, the first tale, the formula tale, seems to be largely limited in distribution to India. Since the tale is not found to any degree outside of India, we can legitimately argue that whatever the tale means, it may well refer exclusively to Indic culture. But if AT 2030B is basically an Indian tale, the subgenre of cumulative formula tales is not. Such tales are found in African and European traditions (though evidently not in native North or South American traditions). What is significant in this connection is the fact that AT 2030B is a radical departure from the structural norm of standard cumulative tales. Let me explain. In the vast majority of cumulative tales involving chains of inter-related actions or "members," the tension is built up by piling "lacks" upon one another. A needs B, but can't obtain B unless he first obtains C. He cannot obtain C unless or until he first obtains D, etc. The tension is released when—and only when—a final lack is liquidated which sets in motion a whole series of intervening lacks being liquidated so that the initial lack can then be liquidated as well. Accordingly in Aarne-Thompson tale type 2030, The Old Woman and her Pig, the woman cannot get her pig to jump over the stile until a cow gives milk for the cat, the cat threatens to kill a rat, the rat gnaws a rope, the rope might hang a butcher, the butcher might kill an ox, the ox might drink water, the water might quench fire, the fire might burn a stick, the stick might beat a dog, the dog might bite the original pig which is thereby induced to jump over the stile. The point is that in AT 2030B, the crow cannot eat the sparrow until he cleans his bill. That is the original lack, a lack of cleanliness in crow. But in this tale, the series of interlocked conditional lacks are never really liquidated. Instead, the crow dies, usually by fire or by being burned, and he never does get to eat with sparrow. In a modest comparative study of this first tale, Agrawal, discussing five versions, including one from Madhya Pradesh, called it a "tragedy," whereas the normal cumulative formula tale that "recoils to previous events" (1962:129) is termed a "comedy." He remarked, "The story of every region ends with the death of the crow. The crow dies by burning himself in fire or by putting the hot sickle on his feathers. It is a 'tragedy'" (1962:132).

What we have here is a fascinating structural oicotype. Not only is this particular formula tale peculiar to India, but its very structure, a departure from formula tale norms, is also oicotypical. What is the significance, if any, of this oicotype? It would seem fairly obvious that the "message" of the tale is that crows cannot eat with sparrows. And the reason is that crows are dirty, so dirty or impure that they can never get clean. The crow, in short, is an untouchable. The series of supposed conditional variables in the tale is analogous to the hierarchical social organization of the caste system. By seeking to liquidate the various lacks, crow is forced to move further and further away from the inter-dining he or she wishes to enjoy with sparrow. Moreover, in almost every link of the chain, the reason why crow cannot fulfill the condition is his basic impurity. His bill might defile the entire river, etc. In the orderly Indic universe, "clean" is at one end, at the top, and "dirty" is at the other, at the bottom. As our first tale starts with the promise of a communal meal, we see that the attempt to have clean and dirty eat together is unsuccessful. We should recall that one of the major types of caste distinctions and rankings are based upon who can eat food prepared by whom else.

A number of basic binary oppositions in our first tale underscore the message articulated above. There is usually an inherent opposition between the dramatis personae. Sparrow is a clean, provident bird, representing high caste; crow is a dirty scavenger bird, representing an untouchable. Novelist Deshpande whose version of the tale omits all mention of crow's activities inside sparrow's house portrays the two birds in slightly different terms: "There's the foolish, improvident, irresponsible, gullible crow; and there's the cautious, self-centered, worldly-wise, dutiful, shrewd sparrow. The survivor is the sparrow, the sparrow who keeps the crow waiting for hours, and finally, in the guise of providing sympathy and shelter, kills the crow" (1988:17). In dream symbolism, we find the traditional contrast: "If one sees a crow . . . it is a bad omen" but "If one sees a sparrow coming out its nest, he will gain honour; if young ones of the sparrow, superiority over others" (Patell 1904-1907:140). Indian scholar Durga Bhagvat seems to be perfectly right when she observes—in speaking about our first tale—that "The sparrow represents the pure caste and the crow represents the Mahar or untouchable caste" (1959:213).

The separation theme may also be signaled by the choice of food dish mentioned in many of the versions of the tale: khichri. This standard Indian fare consists principally of variously colored *dal*, a legume, and white rice—two ingredients that remain separate (Briggs 1920:174). The fact that *dal* cannot mix with rice perhaps foreshadows the idea that sparrows and crows cannot or should not attempt to integrate or dine together.

Another important binary opposition in the tale is that between mouth and anus. In most versions, the initial task is to clean the beak (mouth), while the final denouement consists of crow's getting burned on its buttocks. The mouth-anus opposition is obviously paralleled by a food-feces contrast, although this is perhaps clearer in the second tale of crow and sparrow. The oppositional structure is also defined in terms of water versus fire. Crow begins by searching for water (to clean his dirty beak) but ends by having his beak or butt burned by fire. Although one could certainly argue that both water and fire are purifying agents, it is also true, in terms of the tale, that water is life and fire is death. In that sense, the overall paradigm would confirm that mouth and food are related to life, while anus and feces are related or equated to death. It's not just that the crow cannot eat with sparrow, but it is that his first attempt to do so (to break the inter-dining taboo) results in death.

Implicit in the tales of crow and sparrow is the idea of immutability. A crow cannot be anything but a crow, in the same way that an untouchable cannot be anything but an untouchable. Thus the very attempt of the crow to remove his "dirtiness" is in the Indian context itself a source of humor. Proverbs attest to the crow metaphor in this connection. Consider such Tamil proverbs as "Even if a crow bathe in the Ganges, it will not become a swan" and "Even if a crow is washed and bathed thrice a day, it will not become a white crane" (Jensen 1986:72-3, nos. 677, 686). In both cases, the crow seeks through bathing to become more like another bird, a clean bird, but the crow's basic nature cannot be altered by bathing.

The first tale of crow and sparrow may be a play upon two different kinds of pollution or defilement. One is *ascribed* ritual defilement, while the other is *situational* ritual defilement, according to one classification scheme proposed (Singh 1966:132):

> An individual, unlike other defilers, has two ritual levels, one ascribed and the other situational. The ascribed ritual level which he acquires by birth is the ritual level of his caste. The situational level is his ritual state in which he is found at a

particular moment of time. Whereas the ascribed ritual remains the same all the time, the situational level keeps on changing from one end of the ritual scale for an individual to the other.

In terms of our folktale, the crow has "ascribed" ritual defilement and, therefore, cannot succeed in bettering or removing his polluted or polluting state. The irony is that the foolish crow behaves as though he could remove his ascribed status through individual effort. Presumably, the audience knows that he cannot.

The second tale of crow and sparrow also displays oicotypical features. If it is truly an Indic set of versions of Aarne-Thompson tale type 123/333, there are clearly features that occur only in the Indic texts. A. K. Ramanujan (1987:121) labeled the folktale as one "told to children of toilet-training age (3-5)." In a second discussion of this tale, Ramanujan remarked that "Children laugh a lot at this story—especially at the crow filling the sack with her excrement, Sparrow's children getting their hands dirty with it, and Sparrow's revenge" (1989:257). After noting that psychoanalysts would likely interpret the tale in terms of anal eroticism, Ramanujan mused, "The Crow and Sparrow story, I've often thought, was part of our toilet training." Certainly the transformation of food into feces is not found in most versions of Aarne-Thompson tale types 123 and 333, although to be sure there are toilet training aspects of the European tales. . . . Little Red Riding Hood in oral (as opposed to the prettified censored versions of Perrault and the Grimms) versions, makes her getaway from the wolf by claiming she needs to go outside to defecate, a device also found in the Chinese, Japanese and Korean versions of the tale (cf. Dundes 1989).

Ramanujan's Kannada version of the tale ends with the crow flying away in pain cawing "Ka! Ka!" In Bengali, the crow is called Kak or Pat-Kak (Mitra 1926-1927:143). The name may be a matter of ono-matopoeia in terms of the sound made by the crow, but it is also strikingly similar to *kaka* an Indo-European root for excrement (Mann 1984:461). Buck (1949:275) lists *kakka* as a nursery word for feces.

Regardless of the possible validity of the linguistic similarity of the crow's cry, the crow's name, and the term for feces, the association of the crow with feces cannot be denied. In the second tale, the crow defecates inside the house—as we shall see, the custom is to defecate outside the house. The crow defecates in a space earmarked for food, and thus violates one of the cardinal rules of Indian culture: mixing food and feces.

What are the associations of crows in India? The crow is "an unclean eater" (Roy 1927-1931:525), meaning that it eats carrion or dead animals (Singh 1966:131). Crows are polluting "for they prey on dead animals" (Saraf 1971:19). Anthropologist Srinivas noted that the crow is a scavenger bird and is everywhere associated with death and accordingly is "impure" (1952:106).

Crows also represent the spirits of the dead, and, as a consequence of this folk belief, food may be thrown on the roof as offerings to the crows (spirits of the dead). "Every Hindu, from the highest Brahman to the lowest Sweeper, makes offerings to crows after a death" (Stevenson 1920:187).

> Food is thrown on the roof of the house and the crows called
> to come eat it. . . It is only when they see the crows
> devouring the food that has been thrown on to the roof that the
> women of the house feel sure that the spirit of the dead man
> is happy; and it is often pathetic to hear the way the women
> call over and over again to the birds, beseeching them to come
> and eat, for it is only through these birds (the chief scavengers
> of India) that the broken-hearted mother or widow can gain
> any assurance that their lost loved one is not still wandering
> forlorn in outer darkness and misery. (Stevenson 1920:188; cf.
> Dubois 1906:487; Fuchs 1950:32)

Untouchability is also a factor in crow folklore. "Physical touch of a crow causes impurity" (Saraf 1969:169). "The crow is considered unclean. . . Better caste men and women consider it a duty to take a purifying bath or at least to change the wearing apparel if he or she has accidentally touched a crow. The belief in the untouchability of the crow . . . has been of some help to them in the struggle for existence" (Roy 1927-1931:534-535). Speaking of the untouchables known as Candalas, Briggs (1953:30) remarked "Among men they are what the crow is among birds." In the state of Jaipur in 1911, "a sweeper was required to wear a crow's feather on his turban to show his unclean caste" (O'Malley 1932:150).

The association of the crow with excrement is even more explicit. In Harper's important study of ritual pollution among the Novik Brahmans in the area around Sagar in the Malnad part of South India, we are told: "Although the feces of all animals except cows cause defilement to Haviks, crow droppings are particularly defiling." A Brahman defiled in this way "must take a thousand and one baths, which he accomplishes by pouring water over himself through a sieve—the water coming through each hole counts as a separate bath" (Harper 1964:169; Srinivas offers a similar account of this riddle/impossible task (1952:107). Earlier Mitra (1898:67) had noted: "If a crow passes ordure on the body of a person, it is believed he will fall ill. The person, thus rendered unclean, must purify himself by sprinkling Ganges water on his body and, thereby, avert the evil or illness which would otherwise overtake him" (cf. also Mitra 1889-1892:585).

There is yet another reason why the crows are considered impure. They eat leftovers. "The crows eat what the boys and girls have left" (Roy 1927 1927-1931:533). As we shall discuss later in this essay, leftovers (food and other materials) are extremely polluting. For this reason, eating leftovers means eating pollution (cf. Dubois 1906:184).

Other relevant data includes a Gond creation myth in which the Great God "bathed himself, and out of the dirt from his body he made a crow" (Elwin 1936:13, 233). The black color of the crow might also support its undeniable association with feces—as is the case of the black raven in Europe (cf. Blum 1931:365). Pigmentation is part of caste—the term *Varna* means 'color' and skin coloration manifests social hierarchy too: "clean" white at the top; "dirty" black at the bottom. "Trust neither a black Brahman nor a white Noleya" cautions a Kanarese proverb (Edwardes 1904-1907:322). There seems no reason to doubt that the crow is "the pariah among Birds" (Dubois 1906:476). The point is that all these associations are understood by Indians—at least to some extent—when they hear the tales of crow and sparrow.

Armed with a knowledge of the crow's associations with excrement as well as its identification as a kind of untouchable, we are better able to interpret our tales. The very fact that crow asks to be admitted inside sparrow's house is cast in a new light—no pun intended. (It is noteworthy how often in the second tale that sparrow is described as being "inside," as opposed to crow being "outside"!) Keep in mind that:

> The Mahar of every class and of every occupation is untouchable, that is to say, none of the twice-born classes of Hindu can touch him or be touched by him without contracting ceremonial uncleanness; and there is no entry for him onto the shrines of the gods which are worshipped by those Hindus. A

Mahar cannot enter the house of a twice-born man without
carrying defilement into it. (Robertson 1938:8)

We also know that while "giving foodgrains or clothing to a people of
a caste other than one's own was not uncommon. . . not a single case of
sheltering in one's own house or nursing an ill person of a caste other
than one's own was recorded" (Karve 1959:149). What this all means is
that sparrow's reluctance to admit crow to her home is perfectly
reasonable and that allowing crow to enter was contrary to normal caste
etiquette. Crow's response of eating food during the night and defecating
in the food container is, thus, in part, a parable of what can happen if
one violates the caste norms—that is, one's home is defiled.

The particular stalling device employed by sparrow to keep crow
waiting outside is itself of possible psychological interest. Sparrow
responds to crow's request for succor by claiming that she must first feed
or bathe her nestlings. It is only after the sparrow has completed all of
her responsibilities to her young (and sometimes also to her husband) that
she finally allows crow to enter her dwelling. Crow's voraciously eating
food during the night and defecating in the food container, or in some
versions of eating the nestlings, strongly suggests a theme of sibling
rivalry. If we regard the crow as the older child, we can interpret this
element as an infant's or child's eye view of what happens when he or
she is "replaced" by a new baby sibling. Mother no longer has any time
to take care of the needs of the older child. Even the husband can serve
as a rival for the mother's attention from the child's perspective. In this
context, the act of defecation takes on special significance. As one
psychoanalyst phrased it, "Many children revert to unclean habits when
a rival appears" (Landauer 1939:423). By defecating, crow or the older
child regresses to a period or act of infancy that is more or less
guaranteed to get mother's attention. We also know that in Indian
children's humor, the high point of the tales children tell to one another
"is always the description of the deposition of the feces, and the more
pure and sacred the chosen place, the more hilarity greets the teller"
(Vatuk 1970:275). Many children have experienced the dismay of dealing
with an unwanted younger sibling and can relate to the pleasure in
defecating in a forbidden place such as a food container.

One significant detail common to both of our tales of crow and
sparrow is the burning of crow at the end. In this context, the fact that
sparrow and crow engage in a chili-eating contest in one version may be

relevant. Chilis, hot chilis, have an indisputable effect on the digestive system including the anal area, often causing a "burning" sensation during evacuation. So in terms of the mouth-anus opposition, chilis taken in at the mouth result in the anus being burned when they come out. There is a relevant Hindi proverb: "If you eat fire, you'll shit sparks" (Shukla 1992:69, 115).

Even more important, fire or burning is a highly regarded device thought to be able to remove pollution or impurity. Fire is definitely seen as being a purificatory force (Dubois 1906:520-552; Narasimhan 1992:118). Someone expelled from a caste could be readmitted by submitting to an ordeal whereby "his tongue is slightly burnt with a piece of heated gold; he is branded on different parts of his body with red-hot iron" (Dubois 1906:42). One form of customary punishment consisted of burning the accused's buttocks by means of heated tongs (Darling 1934:80). Allegedly in ancient India, if a Sudra had sat down next to someone high born, he would be punished "after being branded on his hip or his backside be cut off" (Kamble 1982:17-18). In our second tale, inasmuch as crow has defiled sparrow's home by defecating in the food vessels, it is perfect *lex talionis* to have the offending body part punished, namely by burning the buttocks or by shoving a hot piece of metal up the anus. (As feces that came out of the anus defiled the home, sparrow was indulging in the appropriate punishment by shoving a hot object into crow's anus.)

The antiquity of the negative image of crows is attested. Although our two tales of crow and sparrow are not related to a Jataka tale in which a greedy crow tries to take food from a pigeon who lives in a kitchen—the cook notices the crow and plucks out his feathers and dips the naked crow into a mixture of ginger, salt, cumin and sour buttermilk, the crow is certainly punished. He dies, and the cook flings him "on the dust-heap" (Cowell 1973: I:112-114; III:248-250; cf. Grey 1990:48-49, 54). Much closer to our two tales is a curious narrative reported by Hertel that involves a crow seeking shelter from storm and rain. He asks to stay overnight. In the morning, the host finds that the crow has dropped an excrement before departing (Hertel 1907:51-52,57).

The documented association of crow with excrement would seem to support Ramanujan's intuition that the second tale is about toilet training. Ramanujan believed the story seemed to favor crow's perspective—at least up to the final act of revenge:

> I have always felt a certain ambivalence, and so did the tellers and the other children, about Sparrow. She is not generous or hospitable; she keeps Crow waiting in the rain. Because of her grudging hospitality, one feels Sparrow somewhat deserves Crow's untidy return. Children laugh gleefully at Sparrow's discomfiture and enjoy Crow's filling the sack up with nightsoil. (Ramanujan 1989:257)

Certainly in the first tale of crow and sparrow, the tale is told from crow's point of view. It is very much crow's story and one cannot help but be sympathetic to crow's plight. That sparrow rather than crow is punished in some versions suggests a possible shift in attitudes toward crow and untouchability.

In the second tale, crow represents freedom with respect to toilet behavior. Crow can defecate inside, where he or she sleeps, and get away with it. At the same time, there is a moral twist inasmuch as crow is severely punished for its anal indiscretion by having its buttocks burned or by being burned alive. In a society where there is such an emphasis upon keeping food and feces apart, there can only be humor in sparrow's children mistaking feces for food or finding feces where food ought to be.

One of the important lessons that all children in India must learn is not to mistake food for feces or feces for food. The mouth and anus must be kept separate (although in the tale it is interesting that censored forms of the narrative have the crow burn its mouth rather than its anus, a substitution which suggests symbolic equivalence). The opposition between mouth and anus is reported in Tamilnadu where a house can be perceived in body-like terms. A man admonished a recently hired servant boy whom he saw sweeping water toward the front door of the house by saying "You ass! Take the water that way [pointing toward a rear door]. Do you defecate through your mouth?" (Daniel 1984:152).

Is there truly a discrepancy between Durga Bhagvat's claiming that our first tale is really about caste and A. K. Ramanujan's suggestion that our second tale is really about toilet training? I submit that both of these scholars are right—for the tales are about caste, untouchability, *and* toilet training. I shall try to demonstrate this in the sections of this essay to follow.

## The Bodily Origin of Caste

Is there any evidence to support the contention that there is some kind of logical or psychological connection between caste/untouchability and the posterior portion of human anatomy? Is it anything more than mere assertion to claim that toilet training in India is inextricably bound up with the particulars of caste behavior including untouchability?

I believe there are a number of clues pointing to the anal origin of caste, clues that Indologists have either failed to observe or have consistently ignored. The most blatant clue is provided by the nearest thing we have to an "origin" myth of caste. This is an oft-quoted "Hymn of Man" from the *Rig Veda* (circa 2000-1500 B.C. though the passage in question may have been a late addition), which Dutt (1968:31) has called "the Magna Carta of the caste system." Most discussions of caste in India in fact begin with citation of this passage (*Rig Veda* 10.90.12), which describes how primordial man is divided: "His mouth became the Brahman; his arms were made into the Warrior, his thighs the People, and from his feet the Servants were born" (O'Flaherty 1981:31). This would appear to be a form of Motif A 1211, Man made from creator's body, a motif typologically analogous to the so-called Ymir myth, Motif A 614, Universe from parts of creator's body, or Motif A 614.1, Universe from parts of man's body (cf. Lincoln 1975). This motif is more specific than Motif A 1641, Origin of castes, and Motif A 1618, Origin of inequalities among men, both of which, however, are reported only in India. As with all myths, there are variants, e.g., Brahmans come from the mouth, warriors from the arms, commoners from the penis, the Shudras from the feet (Smith 1989:248).

The critical point is that these four *Varna* castes are, metaphorically at least, given a bodily origin and are ranked hierarchically, literally from top to bottom, from head to foot, with Brahmans at the top and Servants, or Sudras, at the bottom. We may remind the reader that there is no fifth group, the untouchables, who undoubtedly rank outside and beneath the four named groups.

Now to be sure, all Indologists and anthropologists specializing in India know full well that this idealized and somewhat literary oversimplified "charter for belief" for caste, to use Malinowski's definition of myth, in no way accounts for the hundreds of different caste and subcaste groups actually living throughout India. Nevertheless, the basic paradigm of the four Varnas plus untouchables still carries some cultural weight in Indic society to the extent that Brahmans continue to occupy the highest ranking of any caste as opposed to Sudras and untouchables who are relegated to the bottom rungs of the caste ladder.

But we have not yet solved the puzzle of the origin of the untouchables. If the four Varna castes are said to have a bodily origin, can we assume that the untouchables may also have come from the body of primordial man? And if so, what part of the body might that be? To put the questions another way, could there be or was there ever a fifth Varna caste comprising the untouchables?

One reason to believe there may once have been a fifth Varna caste comes from the ritual use of the number five in Indic culture. The Hindus recognized five elements: earth, water, fire, ether, and wind (Dubois 1906:555; cf. Kirfel 1951). Brahma "was born with five heads" (Dubois 1906:545); local customary law is administered by a body of five men called a *panchayat* (O'Malley 1932:37). The famous literary collection of folktales is the *Panchatantra,* and a traditional scientific treatise on astronomy called "The Science of the Five Birds" (Ayyar 1982:102-103). An ancient dice game involves five dice (Eggeling 1894:106). The number five recurs in countless daily rituals. "Cowdung is a potent protective article. By hanging five balls of cowdung on a pole, grain is protected from being stolen by thieves" (Briggs 1953:512). After participating in a cremation ritual, the individuals involved "threw some cow dung water on these tools with the fifth finger of the left hand" (Freeman 1979:126). These few examples are meant to be illustrative and not an exhaustive demonstration of the ritual status given to the number five. I should note that I am not the first to see a possible penchant for *pancha* in India. Italian scholar Gabriella Eichinger Ferro-Luzzi (1977:512) pointed out that "The number five seems to be the culturally most favored number in India." She even suggested that preference for five may derive from the counting of the fingers of just one hand: "This is perhaps not accidental in India, where the left hand is considered impure" (1977:512).

In any case, whether I am right or wrong about the number five in India, it is a fact that there is an empirically observable folk tendency to regard the untouchables as a fifth caste—a tendency marked by the use of the term *panchamas*, meaning "fifth," that is, below the Shudra or fourth caste (Singh 1913:376n; Kamaraju and Ramana 1984:362). Not everyone accepts the use of the term panchamas. (See Charsley 1996:5). "Sometimes they [untouchables] were called 'the fifth caste,' but most

(Brahman) authorities rejected even that, insisting that they were outside the Aryan social order altogether!" (Gandhi 1982-1983:258).

There is textual or literary authority for the exclusion of untouchables. Manu said "All of those castes who are excluded from the world of those who were born from the mouth, arms, thighs, and feet (of the primordial Man) are traditionally regarded as aliens, whether they speak barbarian languages or Aryan languages" (Doniger 1991:241, [10:45]). But Manu also says, "If a man of one birth hurls cruel words at one of the twice-born, his tongue should be cut out, for he was *born from the rear-end*" (Doniger 1991:181-182 [8:370], my italics). Doniger offered the following in her explanatory note: "'From the rear-end' (jaghanya) means literally 'from the buttocks' and refers to cosmogonies in which certain human groups are born of that part of the creator; figuratively, it means 'last, lowest, vile'" (1991:182, n.270). There are other allusions in Manu to men "of the rear castes" (Doniger 1991:191 [8:365, 366]), and Doniger has in an earlier work discussed Brahma's anal creation, which would, in her earthy words, make man "a cosmic turd" (O'Flaherty 1976:140). There is also the standard myth in which Pragapati creates the immortal gods by breathing upwards, and mortals, all castes presumably, by his "downward breathings" (Eggeling 1894: 150; 1897:289), an anal creation myth noticed by Ernest Jones as early as 1914 (Jones 1951:279). (For a technical philological discussion of "down-breathing" or *apāna* as "anus breath" or flatus from the lower bowel, see Ewing 1901; cf. also Dutt's citation (1968:90) from the twelfth book of the *Mahabharata,* which gives the origin of the Nishadas, a pariah people, one of several belonging to a would-be 'fifth' varna, as deriving from the verb *nishida,* meaning "sit"; for more conventional myths explaining the origin of untouchables, see Deliège 1989).

One of the most curious yet revealing origin myths concerning untouchables is a highly Christianized pseudo-biblical account purporting to explain how sweepers or scavengers came into the world. Here is the narrative as it appeared in a late nineteenth-century missionary periodical:

> Adam and Eve, though clothed in flesh, were innocent as yet of the grosser needs of the body. They had no wants, save to contemplate the glory of the Almighty, singing, "There is no God, save God." The Lord was pleased with His handiwork, and commanded all His angels to worship Adam and Eve as their masters. All the angels obeyed save Satan, who refused,

saying adroitly, "Hast thou not taught me that there is no God save God? Thee will I worship, but none other." Then the Almighty was angered, and sternly charged Satan to kneel down before Adam on pain of everlasting punishment. Satan was afraid, and affected to submit. Nevertheless guile and rancor were in his heart as he entered Paradise, where the seraph hosts were adoring Adam. "Give ear, ye dullards," cried Satan; "how long will ye be content to continue fasting? Behold the ears of corn how they ripen and grow yellow! Shall we ever despise God's bounty? Nay, rather let us eat that the ears wither not, neither fall to the ground, serving no man." Then Satan gave the ear of corn to Adam and Eve and all the angels, and all ate. The earthly food turned to ordure in their bodies. So it was that the earth and steps of heaven were defiled.

As a consequence of all this, according to the myth, the Lord created scavengers to cleanse the earth and steps of heaven. (Scott 1898:258)

We are a long way from the Garden of Eden and the famous apple (which is not actually specified—the forbidden fruit is not named in Genesis 3:3), but what is absolutely fascinating is the possible Indic oicotypification that has taken place. The critical motif is the transformation of food into feces (cf. Eggeling 1897:285). Pure food becomes impure feces and, as such, requires a special workforce to remove it. So the Indianized retelling of Adam and Eve's expulsion from the Garden of Eden becomes an etiological account of the origin of sweepers.

I find this evidence persuasive. If I am correct in assuming that untouchables were "born from the rear-end," to use Manu's words, then we can understand perfectly why they are untouchable. Untouchables are feces; feces cannot or should not be touched; hence untouchables cannot or should not be touched.

The metaphorical use of the body to distinguish purity from impurity, specifically employing the head as symbol for purity and the anus as a symbol for the opposite, can be demonstrated outside of caste origin myths. If a Brahman becomes a mendicant near the end of his life, this is supposed to guarantee:

> that his soul will pass out through one of the upper apertures of his body, such as nose, eyes, or mouth. But it is better still

> if the soul leaves the body by the *Brahmarandhra* (the soft
> part of the skull, which is the last to join up in the case of
> infants), and so, after death, the Sannyasi's skull is often
> broken there by a blow from a conch-shell. . . But the soul of
> a wicked man passes out by the lower apertures of the body,
> and by so doing acquires such defilement that endless
> purifications are necessary. (Stevenson 1920:139)

The fontanelle is, of course, located higher on the body, being at the very top of the head, than the nose, eyes, or mouth. (One is tempted to speculate if a similar metaphysical thought system might underlie the widespread prehistoric practice of trephination.) The critical issue is that holiness depends upon which hole serves as the soul's final exit—high holes equal purity; lower holes signify defilement.

The cultural logic is also manifested in a Brahman Sannyasis' funeral ceremonies. First the body is put in a grave which is filled with salt to make the head immovable. Then coconuts are broken on the head until the skull is completely fractured "so as to free the *prana* (life) which is believed to be imprisoned in the skull" (Dubois 1906:539, n.2), a practice which may be parallel to that of breaking coconuts on lingams as a substitute for heads (Dubois 1906:541). Dubois also described a practice that "consists of holding the breath for such a length of time that the soul, forced to depart from the body, makes a passage for itself through the top of the head and flies off to reunite itself to Parabrahma" (1906:535-536).

There seems to be a consistent pattern whereby the top (pure) is contrasted to the bottom (impure) and whereby the front (pure) is contrasted with the back (impure). We remarked above on the sweeping instructions with respect to front and back doors, but there is other supporting evidence. Food should be taken "from the front towards the back" (Eggeling 1894:402; 1900:425). In funeral rites once again, the Brahman who represents the dead man's ghost "may not enter the house by the front door but only by the back" (Srivinas 1984:163). Translating this, we have death being forced to use the back door or anus. (For compelling evidence of the back door-anus equation in India, see Kripal 1995:287-288).

Is there any other persuasive evidence supporting the bodily origin of castes and untouchability? In South India, a longstanding distinction between left-hand castes and right-hand castes has stimulated considerable debate (Dumont 1980:367-368). Strangely enough, many of the scholars who have written on left- and right-hand castes (e.g., Kearns 1876: Zimmerman 1974: Khare 1976b) fail to remark on the obvious culturewide associations of the left hand with the impurity resulting from using it to clean oneself after defecation (but cf. Beck 1973:395; and Obeysekere 1975:464). Appadurai goes so far as to label "the metaphor of the vertically divided social body" as an example of what is termed a *root paradigm* 1974:221). This is an elegant structural descriptive phrase, but it hardly reveals the underlying psychological basis of this body-based distinction.

Dubois (1906:237-240) gave no less than twenty-three rules "to be observed by Brahmans when answering the calls of nature." He specifically remarked:

> It is only the left hand that may be used on these occasions. It would be thought unpardonably filthy to use the right hand. It is always the left hand that is used when anything dirty has to be done, such as blowing the nose, cleaning the ears, the eyes, etc. The right hand is generally used when any part of the body above the navel is touched, and the left hand below that. (1906:239 n.1)

Noteworthy in Dubois's detail is the coupling of the right hand with the upper part of the body and left hand with the lower part. This suggests that the pure paradigm includes top, front, right, whereas the impure includes bottom, back, and left. It is not just that the right hand cannot be used in processes of elimination, but also that the left hand cannot be used to eat with. The right hand is used to touch food but not feces; the left hand is used to touch feces but not food. Dumont reminds us (1980:49) that in Tamil, the left hand is called the "hand of filth."

Even the nostrils of the nose were subject to the left-right dichotomy. In religious exercises, Dubois explained, one was required to inhale through the right nostril and exhale through the left nostril (1906:534-535). Presumably the exhalation through the left nostril is symbolically equivalent to defecation and the consequent wiping with the left hand, while inhaling through the right nostril was parallel to ingesting food with the help of the right hand. The pure paradigm also includes the semantic opposition between "in" and "out." What goes into the body (food, breath) must be "clean" and "pure." What comes out of the body (feces, exhalation) is culturally defined as "dirty" and "impure."

It should be underscored that the distinction in South India was *not* between left castes and right castes, but left-*hand* castes versus right-*hand* castes. The explicit reference to "hands" makes the association with feces or food unambiguous. In this context, it is easier to understand why the "right Hand faction comprised all the more respectable castes" (Srinivasachari 1930:77) or why the "right-hand sections enjoy certain rights denied to those of the left-hand sections" (Briggs 1953:70 n.2) or why the left-hand castes have "lower social standing" than the other (Briggs 1953:144).

Anthropologist Beck chooses to ignore the "hand" portion of the designations of left-hand and right-hand castes, preferring instead to retain only the "left" and "right" labels (1973:396), but she never does satisfactorily answer the questions she raises: "What underlying principles could have been responsible for maintaining this right-left division for so many centuries?" (1973:394). Nor "why should the untouchables have been the ones who were the most vociferous in the right-left disputes?" (1973:401). She does at least acknowledge that "the dominant peasant caste of the area and their ritual dependents bore the label "right" (1973:393), whereas "subcastes traditionally classified as left . . . are ignored and scoffed at by neutral subcastes and landowners alike" (1973:415).

One of the few writers to see a possible connection between the choice of left-hand and right-hand as designators for castes and toilet practices was Hanumanthan who observed:

> It is also possible that the orthodox Hindus named the heretics as Itankaiyar [left-handed] to denote their low position in society comparable to that of the left hand in the body of a Hindu. It is a custom among Hindus to use the left hand only for filthy purposes such as cleaning the anus after easing the bowels, etc. while the right hand is used for all auspicious and ceremonial purposes. Therefore the right hand is always superior to the left hand for the Hindus. (1979:190-191)

The conclusions we can draw from the above data is that caste and untouchability have roots in the human body and that the body, according to Indic ethnoanatomy, can be binarily divided along a number of axes: top versus bottom; front versus back; right versus left; inside versus outside (cf. Kaushik 1976:279, 282). These dichotomies are absolute. The top "cleanest" caste supposedly came from the head, while the bottom "dirtiest" caste supposedly came from the feet (or anus). The basic point is that the head must be kept separate from the feet; the mouth must be kept separate from the anus; or to put it another way, food must be kept separate from feces. It is the persistent obsessive fear that the top, clean mouth might be contaminated or defiled from the bottom, the dirty anus with its feces, that underlies and permeates the entire caste system. This explains why a higher caste cannot accept food from the hands of a lower caste—for fear of contamination. Feet (and what is worn on the feet) are dirty because they are in contact with the outside ground where feces may lurk.

One of the worst insults in India consists of being struck on the head with a shoe. It is considered "very ignominious to be slapped with a shoe" (Fuchs 1950:334). "Beating with shoes is a great indignity in India, especially on the head, since that is the most honorable part of the body. Shoebeating is a more humiliating punishment than beating with a stick" (Emerson 1930:45). "Being beaten with shoes is regarded in this culture as the most degrading kind of punishment" (Vatuk 1970:276). "According to Hindu belief, the head is the highest and purest part of the body, the feet the lowest and most defiling. To place a person's foot on another's head or to hit a person with shoe are great insults" (Freeman 1979:85n). "To be struck on the head by another's shoe conveyed a humiliation out of all proportion to the physical hurt" (Carstairs 1957:79). "By far the greatest indignity of all, however, is to be struck with one of the shoes or sandals that Hindus wear. Whoever submitted to such an insult without insisting on receiving satisfaction would be excluded from his caste. The mere threat of such an insult is often sufficient to provoke a criminal prosecution" (Dubois 1906:330). There are even reports of diverse techniques employed, e.g., using a shoe soaked in water for three days because it makes more noise when it lands on the victim so that "even people far away can hear that there's a beating in progress" (Shukla 1992:37).

The conventional wisdom among India experts is that shoes or sandals are made of leather, that is, the skin of a dead animal. "The rule about shoes is that they should be taken off before entering a house or a temple, and before drinking water or tea, because they are made of the skin of a dead animal and so are impure; their removal has no ritual significance" (Stevenson 1920:270). Anthropologist Srinivas stated:

The seriousness of beating with sandals arises from the fact

> that only Untouchables handle leather, and, when a high caste
> man is beaten with sandals, he becomes an outcaste and may
> be readmitted to caste only after he has undergone an
> expensive ceremony of purification. (Srinivas 1959:205)

I am sure the "leather" explanation has some merit, some truth
to it, but I do not think it is the full explanation for the horror of being
touched by a shoe. In the present context, I suspect it is the fact that the
shoe comes into necessary contact with the space outside the home, this
space being contaminated with feces, spittle, and other impurities. Thus
shoes must be removed before entering a temple or house to avoid
bringing "outside" feces "inside" these structures. "Outside" must be
kept separate from "inside" as in our second crow and sparrow folktale.
It is what I might term the "fear of feces," which lies at the very heart
of the entire Indic caste system. This is why placing a shoe on someone's
head is such an insult: the top is defiled by contact with the bottom just
as a Brahman is defiled by contact with an untouchable. In the same
way, not using the left hand to feed the mouth is, symbolically speaking,
precisely and the same rule which forbids lower "dirty" castes from
preparing and serving food to upper "clean" castes.

One more piece of evidence supports the identification of
untouchables with feces. Surely it defies logic to think that it is people
per se who should be considered untouchable. It is rather a case of guilt
or dirt by association. It is feces which is the ultimate untouchable
substance. Therefore, it is those who remove night soil, the sweepers,
and those who remove garbage or refuse (fecal substitutes or surrogates)
who are the individuals or castes deemed "untouchable." Untouchability
may be understood as negative contagious magic if we wish to utilize
Frazer's classic principles of sympathetic magic. O'Keefe has argued that
hierarchy and purity are "magical ideas" (1983:545) in his discussion of
caste. Frazer articulated two principles of sympathetic magic. The first,
homeopathic magic or imitative magic, is based on the idea "that like
produces like, or that an effect resembles its cause" (Frazer 1913:52,
174). The second, the Law of Contact or Contagion, presumes "that
things which have once been in contact with each other continue to act
on each other at a distance after the physical contact has been severed"
(1913:52, 174). It is this second principle of contagious magic that
illuminates untouchability. Since feces is defiling, the untouchable
sweeper who handles it is inevitably defiled. Moreover, anything the
untouchable later touches may become defiled. This is why if an

untouchable or just his water vessel touches a well, the entire contents of the well becomes polluted. This is what I mean by negative contagious magic.

It is true, however, that untouchables are "untouchable" by birth, long before they have become professional sweepers. So the "origins" of the sweepers' untouchability cannot be attributed to handling feces. Still, the origin "myth," which has untouchables born from the anus, would tend to equate untouchables with feces—in terms of body origins, that is, from the back, from the lower part of the body, from the anus, which is cared for by the left hand. The sweepers' handling of feces is thus more of a confirmation or corroboration of their untouchable status than a cause. It is of interest that many of the activists who are disturbed by the existence of untouchability are particularly upset by the fact that male and female sweepers typically carry buckets of nightsoil on their *heads* (Gandhi 1964:68) in the absence of other means of removing this material. From these activists' perspective, carrying feces on one's head constitutes an utterly demeaning activity, more or less analogous to being hit on the head with a shoe! There was even an "Enquiry Committee on Scavenging Conditions" established in October 1957 "to put an end to the degrading practice of scavengers having to carry night-soil in buckets or baskets on the head" (Malkani 1965:119; Searle-Chatterjee 1979:276). It was proposed to abolish "head-loads" by using wheelbarrows instead (Malkani 1965:125). However, wheelbarrows proved to be too heavy for female scavengers to push and were too wide to negotiate narrow lanes (Isaacs 1965:54).

If the reader is at all persuaded that there might possibly be a connection between "untouchability" and feces on the basis of the data presented thus far, he should also realize that entire books, monographs, and articles devoted to the question of "untouchability" have made no mention whatsoever of feces or a hypothetical anal erotic origin of the custom. One analyst asks most tentatively in small print buried in an obscure footnote: "We may ask: Does a rational assessment of status in terms of avoidance of physical contact with polluting substances such as human emissions underlie all, or many, or few, or any of the avoidances of the 'intrinsically' polluted phenomena noted?" (Stevenson 1954:55 n.2). This is euphemistic academese, but it does at least hint at the argument of this essay.

## Defecation Habits

Indoor plumbing is a relatively recent innovation in most parts of the world. Traditionally, individuals were obliged to go outside of their dwellings to urinate or defecate. Even in the United States, rural people were accustomed to using outhouses, referring to latrines located some distance from the house proper where one slept and ate. In India, the situation was somewhat different because for reasons that will be explained, there was a deep-seated reluctance to use latrines. Instead, individuals were expected to go to a nearby open area, e.g., a field, preferably near water so that they could cleanse themselves after defecation. Otherwise, they had to carry water-vessels with them with sufficient water to cleanse the buttocks and hands. Sometimes plain earth was used to clean the hands. Since the left hand is employed (rather than the right), it was subject to more stringent cleansing rules. "He then cleanses his left hand ten times with clay, his right hand seven times, and lastly both together five times" (Stevenson 1920:212). "Vishnu first gives the rules for cleansing oneself after voiding excrement—one cleans the left hand ten times, the right seven" (Orenstein 1968:123). Sometimes both earth and water were utilized. As a result of everyone's defecating in public, it was not uncommon to see fecal deposits outside in plain view.

Many foreign observers could not help but notice the cumulative effect of public defecation. The situation obtained in both urban and rural settings. "Most Hindu villages of the Nimar are dirty and unsanitary . . . . The village lanes are often so narrow that no cart can pass through them, they are mere footpaths along which runs the gutter water and into which is emptied every sort of muck, rubbish and excrements" (Fuchs 1950:343). It was apparently even worse where the low castes and untouchables lived: ". . . the narrow, tortuous lanes through their quarters are filthy, slippery, full of animal and human excreta. . . . I have often seen the Sweeper's pigs devouring human excreta in the village lanes and court-yards and then licking the cooking pots of the Balahis laying around before the houses!" (Fuchs 1950:343). In the Punjab, we have a similar account: "We set out at 9:30 and, skirting the village and its landlord mansions, picked our way along a dusty road shamelessly defiled by menials too lazy to step across the road into the fields for their necessary occasions" (Darling 1934:3). British administrators tried, in vain, to change these habits in adults: "The people must be taught to abandon bad customs, such as . . . relieving themselves round the village like dogs" (Darling 1934:66).

Some readers might assume that this is no longer the case in the late twentieth century, but it is. "On a journey through India, one's senses can be continually reviled by the lack of general hygiene—children urinating in the gutters, men defecating along the roadside, piles of discarded rubbish dumped in public places" (Baker 1990:49). As one western traveler in India put it, "the textbooks had said nothing about . . . the piles of excrement" (Muehl 1950:31).

It should be noted that it wasn't just foreigners who were shocked by the public display of feces. Indians saw the same scene and several, especially those who managed to attain some sort of objectivity, e.g., by living or being born outside of India, were equally appalled by such scenes. Gandhi himself expressed displeasure on more than one occasion at the practice of public defecation. While attending a Congress Party meeting in Calcutta in 1901, he was so horrified that he tried to do something about it:

> There were only a few latrines, and the recollection of their stink still oppresses me. I pointed it out to the volunteers. They said pointblank: "That is not our work, it is the scavenger's work." I asked for a broom. The man stared at me in wonder. I procured one and cleaned the latrine. . . . But that was not all. Some of the delegates did not scruple to use the verandas outside their rooms for calls of nature at night. In the morning I pointed out the spots to the volunteers. No one was ready to undertake the cleaning, and I found no one to share the honour with me of doing it. (Gandhi 1954a:275)

Gandhi found similar conditions on a boat bound for Rangoon. "What was an apology for a bathroom was unbearably dirty, the latrines were stinking sinks. To use the latrine one had to wade through urine and excreta or jump over them" (1954a:473). Gandhi's willingness to handle human feces sometimes led to quarrels with his long-suffering wife. During his sojourn in South Africa, Gandhi's law office clerks occasionally stayed with him. They were lodged in rooms with chamber pots. The Indian clerks cleaned their own pots, but a Christian newcomer posed a problem. Gandhi's wife could not bear Gandhi's cleaning the clerk's chamber pot, but then again she could not bear doing it herself (1954a:339).

Other Indians have remarked on defecation habits. After stating "We in India are a fairly clean people in our opinion" and then referring to daily teeth cleaning, mouth rinsing, and washing after urination and defecation, Malkani proceeds to admit, "We have the inveterate habit of sitting anywhere. . . . We do it with ease and indifference as if we have a right to use any place as our very own" (1965:15, 17).

The talented writer V. S. Naipaul has also commented on this aspect of Indian culture. He reported "a young foreign academic" at a dinner party in Delhi who was asked "what was most noticeable about the crowds he had seen in Bombay on his Indian holiday." His answer: "They were doing their 'potties' on the street" (Naipaul 1977:124). But Naipaul had earlier been much more explicit himself: "Indians defecate everywhere. They defecate, mostly, beside the railway tracks. But they also defecate on the beaches; they defecate on the hills; they defecate on the river banks; they defecate on the streets; they never look for cover" (1964:74).

Moreover, attempts by civil authorities to ban defecating in the open have invariably been met with resistance and failure. People who live without toilets ask the legitimate question, "Where should we defecate?" (Kulkarni 1994:22). Environmental sanitation remains a pressing issue. "Hundreds of men, women and children in the country keep defecating in the open—all along the highways, railway lines, airport routes, open grounds/spaces. Women are the worst sufferers. They have to wait all the time to defecate either after sunset or before sunrise" (Kulkarni 1994:22). It turns out that there are public health implications of open-air defecation, especially since many individuals go barefoot. This practice facilitates the incidence of hookworm infection (Kochar et al., 1976:303).

If the reader should for any reason doubt the accuracy of the graphic accounts of Gandhi and Naipaul or wrongly assume that these writers were describing something that existed only in the distant past, let him ponder the following vivid detail provided by a Tamil-speaking Sri Lankan anthropologist carrying out fieldwork in south India. His report of his participation in a pilgrimage involving bathing in a river includes the following:

> The river was called Aruda . . . .In all, over 100,000 pilgrims were either bathing, about to bathe, or had just finished bathing in the river. The rocky/gravelly shores were covered with squatters in the morning twilight. It would have taken an

acrobat to tiptoe his way through the piles of human
excrement, which seemed to be as numerous as the stones and
pebbles that covered the shores. . . . I sludged and slid my
way into the water and quickly immersed myself but once and
returned to the river bank feeling helplessly filthy. I fetched
my comb from my knapsack and let it slide through my
dripping hair. I looked at the comb and saw something brown
adhering to its teeth. I lifted the comb to my nose. It stank of
night soil. . . . The world outside was reduced to a oneness:
It was all shit! (Daniel 1984:262-263; cf. Naipaul 1977:167)

At this point, a western reader might well wonder why public
bathrooms were not constructed. Even the simplest outhouse or latrine
would, in theory, seem to have been potentially helpful. But this is
ethnocentric thinking. For one thing, latrines in India are not like public
or private toilets in the West. Consider the following representative
account written by an untouchable:

During the rains the worst possible punishment was
the visit to the latrine, usually situated at the farthest corner of
the house. The pathway to the latrine was laid with bricks
placed along the entire length. It created its own difficulty
when one had to hold an umbrella in one hand and a water
bowl in the other with no third hand for holding the dhoti/sari
ends safely and sufficiently upward to escape the blotches of
muddy water shot up by the yielding brick pathway. One
would also require a fourth hand to manage a hurricane
lantern at night to visit latrines during the rains. The skill
required was even superior to that displayed by rope dancers
in a circus.

The latrines were veritable hells. They were
ramshackle wooden platforms constructed with only odds and
ends of timber and tin strips, with mounting steps rising
almost to their middle. Mostly a dirty gunny bag would be
hung to serve as the screen. The receptacles below would
normally be a flat-bottomed earthen pot. (Das 1985:10; for an
account of the cleaning of latrines by Bhangies, "the foulest
part of a foul business," see Malkani 1965:9)

But there is a more compelling reason why Indians do not like
to use public latrines, a reason that may be somewhat hard for westerners
to understand. The reason is related to a "theory of left-overs," which

I shall discuss in detail later in this essay. For now, it may be sufficient to say that the Indian folk belief system includes the basic idea that the human body contains various impurities. As expressed in a folk poem, "The human body, under the attractive looking skin is full of blood and flesh and such other stuff; the body contains excreta, faeces, and urine; the nose is full of mucus" (Karve 1962:24). Once any of these substances is emitted from one of the body's seven apertures, the substance becomes automatically defiling—even to the emitter. With this rationale, both men and women believe that it is much more hygienic to visit a new area to defecate than to use the same place over and over again. Re-using a place risks contamination from the results of a previous act of defecation.

Even more critical is the resistance to using a place previously used by someone else! This makes it possible to understand the fierce cultural resistance to western-inspired efforts to introduce latrines and modern plumbing fixtures into rural village India. Villagers "do not like the use of the same latrine by more than one person," since the first person who uses it automatically pollutes it for the second, thus requiring ceremonial purification after every use of the latrine (Fraser 1968: 256-257). Naipaul (1991:246) alluded to this: "The very idea of the latrine was a non-brahman idea: to enter such a polluted place was itself pollution. No old-time brahman would have even contemplated the idea. Good brahmans, traditional brahmans, used open-air sites, a fresh one each time." Actually, there is some empirical ethnographic evidence suggesting that despite statements claiming that new sites are preferable, many individuals tend to return to the same general spot, e.g., typically within a walking time "of three minutes from their homes" in the case of individuals in rural West Bengal (Kochar et al., 1976:302-303).

In addition to the fear of being defiled by using a latrine, there is also the obvious social advantage of defecating in public. Women looked forward to daily trips out of the village to defecate and bathe as a means of escaping from the drudgery of household duties and of indulging in a socially sanctioned opportunity to exchange gossip with other women engaged in the same activity (Fraser 1968:256-257).

The Indian's aversion to using or rather re-using latrines may become clearer if we mention similar attitudes toward western objects such as handkerchiefs and toothbrushes. Both nasal mucus and saliva count as potentially defiling body products or emissions. This is why:

The sight of a foreigner spitting or blowing his nose into a handkerchief and then putting it into his pocket is enough to make them feel sick. According to their notions, it is the politest thing in the world to go outside and blow one's nose with one's fingers and then to wipe them on a wall. (Dubois 1906:239, n.4, 329)

Dubois (1906:240-241) also gave the "rules to be observed when cleaning the teeth." Gandhi spoke of his morning ablutions: "The operation took me thirty-five minutes, fifteen minutes for the toothbrush and twenty for the bath" (1954a:323). But, of course, it is not the same as the Western toothbrush. Hindus will not use the same toothbrush twice because it is permanently polluted by one's own saliva after use on a single occasion (Spratt 1966:145). Here is a report from early in the twentieth century: "They never, of course, use a brush, but break off a twig freshly every day from one or another of about nine specified trees, all of which possess thorns and milky juice. . . . After the teeth are cleaned . . . the twig is broken in half, and the tongue cleansed with one part; then both bits of the twig are thrown away, for the European idea of using the same toothbrush day after day fills a Hindu's mind with horror" (Stevenson 1920:212-213). Here is another account: "The Hindu is horrified at the use of toothbrushes. 'What! use the same brush twice?' She herself uses a twig of the *Neem* tree, no fatter than her own smallest finger, and of course there is a fresh twig for each using" (Sorabji 1908:95).

Just as there are trees whose wood is appropriate for brushing one's teeth, there are apparently trees whose wood is not. In a brief note suggesting that the concept of untouchability also extends to animals and plants, we are told:

Then there are the low-caste trees just like Hiwar (Reongha) which is considered to be a Mahar and Mehndi (Hina) which is a Charamin. Nobody would use sticks of these plants as toothbrush, as being of low caste they would pollute the mouth. They would not use faggots of these plants in the kitchen, as food cooked with their aid would get polluted.
(Lal 1927:338; for more detail about which trees can be utilized as a "clean" source for toothbrushing twigs, see Kane 1974:655.)

There is yet another reason why Hindus object to using the European toothbrush, at least the old-fashioned kind of toothbrush.

Dubois explained that Hindus feel disgust at European practices because "they use for this purpose a brush made with the bristles of a dead animal, and therefore impure, and also because they use the same brush many times, though it has after the first time been defiled by saliva" (Dubois 1906:240, n.3). And what is this dead animal? "Hindus will on no account use European toothbrushes made of pig's bristles. The continued use of Europeans of toothbrushes which have been defiled by saliva is looked on as horrible" (O'Malley 1932:113). And why is the pig so defiling? ". . . the ban on eating domestic pork and fowls rests on their intrinsic pollution, since they are scavengers which eat offal, faeces, and carrion, all of which are highly polluting" (Stevenson 1954:55). "Tame cocks and pigs, unlike wild ones, are forbidden because of their filthy feeding" (Dutt 1968: 158). Not only are domestic pigs considered defiling, but a distinction is made between domestic and wild pigs. The latter is eaten by some castes because wild pigs, unlike domestic pigs, do not eat feces (Fuchs 1950:357). This is why chickens are regarded as unclean: They "eat dirt and put their beaks into our dishes" (Darling 1934:179). This is why some Indians refuse to eat eggs (Darling 1934: 179), and why it was only sweepers who kept chickens (Darling 1934: 138). Once again, we find a cultural connection with feces. And if the reader should think we are too far afield discussing the brushing of teeth as part of our consideration of defecation habits, I would remind him of one of the laws of Manu that states: "When someone has urinated or defecated, *he should rinse his mouth* and wash the orifices of his body" (Doniger and Smith, 1991:114 [5:138] my emphasis). In any event, we find a close parallel in the reluctance to use the same toothbrush twice and to use the same latrine twice.

Besides the handkerchief and the toothbrush, there is one additional well-regarded (by Europeans) hygienic accoutrement which is despised by Hindus and that is the bathtub. We learned from our tales of crow and sparrow that mouth and anus should be kept apart, be kept separate. Yet unless one is willing to dive headfirst into a tub full of water, this simply cannot be accomplished. One sits in a tub which thereby allows water to flow around and over one's genitals and buttocks. Then with the same water, one washes one's face! From a Hindu point of view, this is absolutely disgusting. Even to a westerner—if he or she bothered to think at all about it—the idea of rinsing one's rear end and then using the same water to wash one's face is not particularly pleasant. This may be why some westerners prefer showers to bathing in tubs.

There is also the matter of sharing a tub, e.g., small children may be bathed in succession (or together) in the same water. When writer Salman Rushdie was about to leave Bombay at age thirteen to go to school in England, his mother had reservations partly because of what she understood to be English bathroom customs: "They wipe their bee tee ems with paper only [instead of using water as Indians do]. Also they get into each other's dirty bathwater." (Hamilton 1996:93). Rushdie himself alludes to the same issue in his novel *Midnight's Children*: "For two months we must live like those Britishers? You've looked in the bathroom? No water near the pot. I never believed, but it's true, my God, they wipe their bottoms with paper only!" (1982:110).

This comparison of Indian and Western post-defecation hygiene is by no means unique. Dubois, writing at the beginning of the nineteenth-century, commented on the comparison: "The European habit of using [toilet] paper is looked upon by all Hindus, without exception, as an utter abomination, and they never speak of it except with horror. There are some who even refuse to believe such a habit exists, and think it must be a libel invented out of hatred for Europeans" (1906:239). A Telugu tale or pseudo-myth, entitled "How Englishmen Got the Best Boons Conferred Upon Them," offers a grudging opposing view:

> God was conferring boons. The Englishman was answering a call of nature then, but hearing of it made himself clean at once with a piece of paper that lay by, and running speedily presented himself first. So God conferred upon him the boons of greatness, wealth, superiority, etc.
>
> The Indian also was answering a call of nature then, but though he heard of the bestowal of boons made himself thoroughly clean with water and went. The result was that he was late and lesser benefits in consequence were bestowed upon him.
>
> This is the reason why the Englishmen are superior in power and everything, and the Indians inferior. (Venkataswami 1923:140)

It is noteworthy that this curious piece of traditional folkloristic "self-hate" is specifically tied to defecation habits and that it is expressed in Telugu folklore in unequivocal terms.

But to return to the matter of sharing tubs, we find additional data. Another female expressed her indignation at the use of tubs: "You go dirty into the water from which you expect to come out clean." When the recorder of this comment countered with "bathing in the Ganges," a river full of pollution, the informant continued, "Ah, but that is different . . . that is holy water, however apparently impure, however apparently contaminated, it is holy" (Sorabji 1908:95). (For an updated version of the same argument, see Alley 1994:129-130.) No culture evidently is exempt from ethnocentric blindness! Abundant data attests to the desideratum of keeping anus and mouth apart, specifically from allowing any anal impurity to defile the mouth. Muli, the untouchable whose autobiography Freeman so painstakingly recorded, made an unequivocal statement: "When defecating, we clench our teeth and speak to no one. If we open our mouths, the bad smell enters and weakens our teeth" (Freeman 1979:118). The rule would appear to be that anything which comes out of the anus must at all cost be kept from entering the oral cavity.

## Freudian Theory in India

The disparity between the apparent freedom to defecate at will outside the home with the rigorous taboos concerning the avoidance of pollution defilement of any kind would seem to be appropriate grist for a psychoanalytic mill. Has Freudian theory been applied to India and Indians? And if so, has the Freudian portrait of so-called anal erotic character been utilized?

It is true that one must beware of applying Freudian principles or any western theory wholesale to a nonwestern culture. This all too common practice smacks of ethnocentrism or in the case of India what is often termed "orientalism" (cf. Inden 1986). Among Indian psychologists, there is certainly resentment of aping or replicating Western models of psychology and even pride in "the gradual setting aside of the Freudian model" (Sinha 1986:15, 27, 69-70). A similar sentiment is expressed in Nandy and Kakar's survey of culture and personality in India:

> . . . the basic problem is still the much-discussed dependence
> on conceptual frameworks which are not intrinsic to the
> experience of the society and which tend to straight-jacket all

data-gathering and interpretation within models generated
mainly on the basis of the Western experience . . . but the
days of *traditional* cultural psychology or psychological
anthropology, it seems, are finally over. This is not entirely
a loss. (1980:159, 160)

On the other hand, while one can caution "Great care must be taken in
culture of personality studies to apply an understanding of the practices
of a given society to its cultural situation" (Moudgil 1972:128), one
should not use extreme cultural relativism as an excuse to preclude any
possible application of Freudian insights to nonwestern cultures. (One
could also reasonably argue that India's cultures are part of an
Indo-European continuum and would, therefore, be more likely to be
susceptible of Freudian-style analysis than a non-Indo-European culture
(Banerjee 1944-1945:185)!)

There were earlier—and for that matter there remain—competing
forms of what might generously be called "psychotherapy" in India (cf.
Rao 1978; Neki 1975), and some writers have gone so far as to suggest
that "Western psychotherapy, as it is, is hardly applicable to the
multitudes in India—except for a handful of Westernized Indians living
in large cosmopolitan cities" (Neki 1975:99; cf. Kapani and Chenet
1986). Others feel that if Freudian theory can successfully be culturally
relativized, that is, if the particulars of Indian cultures, especially details
of infant care and child-rearing, can be taken into account, then
psychoanalytic theory may ultimately prove useful in analyzing Indian
culture. The basic question of whether or not psychoanalytic theory is
itself too culture-bound as a western theory to apply to India, or whether
it is indeed flexible enough to accommodate the cultural particularities of
Indian societies, has been the subject of a number of thoughtful
discussions (Roland 1988; Kurtz 1992; Ramanujam 1992). The general
consensus seems to be that with appropriate modification, psychoanalytic
theory can, in fact, be utilized to probe the unconscious behavior and
symbolism of Indians. That is certainly the view held by the writer of
this essay.

Freud himself was immensely pleased at the establishment of a
branch of the psychoanalytic movement in India (Ramana 1964). The
Indian Psycho-Analytical Society was founded in Calcutta in 1922 (Sinha
1966:427). However, there have been relatively few psychoanalytic
studies of Indic cultures. In any event, most of what little psychoanalytic
theory has been applied to Indic materials (Hartnack 1987; Ramanujam

1992) have said virtually nothing about anal erotic themes and even less about caste and untouchability. Even the few Indian psychologists and psychoanalysts willing to consider the possible relationship between so-called anal erotic character and coercive and noncoercive toilet training (Shrivastava 1988) have failed to see any connection whatsoever between toilet training and caste or untouchability. Psychologist Anant who seeks personality differences in various castes suggested that, among Brahmans, ceremonial bathing "might arise from unconscious impulses to play with the feces during infancy," impulses probably connected to the Brahman home environment where strict toilet training is emphasized (1967:388). But he did not analyze untouchability in this context.

The one notable exception is Owen Berkeley-Hill (1879-1944). (For a review of his psychoanalytic writings on India, see Hartnack 1987:236-245.) Berkeley-Hill, trained by Ernest Jones, was known by Freud (Ramana 1964:128). Berkeley-Hill, according to his autobiography (1939:77), believed that when he went to India in the Indian Medical Service in 1907, he was the only recognized psychoanalyst in the entire country. The fact that he married an Indian woman, a native of Malabar (1939:123), may have given him unusual access to Indian cultures (1939:332).

In any case, the identification of possible anal erotic character traits in India may be said to have begun with Berkeley-Hill's pioneering essay, "The Anal-Erotic Factor in the Religion, Philosophy and Character of the Hindus," which appeared in the *International Journal of Psycho-Analysis* in 1921. An earlier essay, "The Psychology of the Anus," published in the *Indian Medical Gazette* in 1913 made almost no allusion to India in his discussion of anal eroticism, which consisted of summarizing the writings of Freud and Jones on the subject. In the 1921 essay, Berkeley-Hill somewhat mechanically applies Freud and Jones's delineations of anal erotic character to Hindu religious ritual. He cites the elaborate and detailed rules governing the prescribed way of defecating and then commented, "In the rules laid down for the performance of excretory acts, we find an abundance of reaction-formations against the material emitted" (1921:326). This reminds me a bit of Devereux's passing remark commenting on the fact that the Mohave Indians wiped their buttocks with their left hand while eating with their right hand, a parallel practice to that found in India. Said Devereux, "the practice of eating with the right hand reflects a defense against cophragous wishes" (1951:405). Possible reaction-formation notwithstanding, it is certainly true that one of the alleged characteristics of anal erotic character is an obsession with minute detail; in scholarship this borders on extreme pedantry. Dubois (1906:31) described India: "Nothing is left to chance; everything is laid down by rule." This feature has also been noted by Naipaul:

> Caste and clan are more than brother-hoods; they define the individual completely. The individual is never on his own; he is fundamentally a member of his group, with a complex apparatus of rules, rituals, taboos. Every detail of behavior is regulated—the bowels to be cleared before breakfast and never after, for instance, the left hand and not the right to be used for intimate sexual contact, and so on. Relationships are codified. (1977:108)

So Berkeley-Hill may have been on the right track, but he said absolutely nothing about caste per se or untouchability, the subject of this essay.

Berkeley-Hill's 1921 essay was totally ignored by Indologists and, to this day, is rarely if ever cited by them or by anthropologists specializing in India. To be sure, it is not the least bit unusual for Indologists and anthropologists to ignore psychoanalytic writings on subjects of supposedly mutual interest. Even G. Morris Carstairs, an analyst whose childhood was spent in India and whose book *The Twice Born: A Study of a Community of High-Caste Hindus*, published in 1957, remains a classic and arguably the best single psychoanalytic study of India ever written, fails to mention Berkeley-Hill or his essay. It is not until 1966 with the appearance of P. Spratt's *Hindu Culture and Personality: A Psycho-Analytic Study* that we finally get an appreciation of Berkeley-Hill's efforts (See, however, Lewis 1992).

Spratt, in his chapter entitled "The Anal Factor," recapitulated Berkeley-Hill's argument before taking issue with it. "During infancy the early positive interest in faeces is repressed and replaced by a reaction formation against dirt. Hindus show this conspicuously. The chief psychical impulse in the observance of caste is the fear of pollution" (Spratt 1966:206). Then, after recapitulating the three principal traits associated with the Freudian notion of anal character: orderliness, miserliness, and obstinacy, Spratt claimed that "Berkeley-Hill seems to be mistaken on some points" (1966:208). Spratt's critique of the standard picture of anal-erotic character included: "Obstinacy is not typical of Hindus: on the contrary, they are inclined to be easily suasible. . . .

Orderliness is not typical of Hindus. . . ." (1966:209). Spratt continued, ". . . cowdung and cow's urine are used every day by millions for domestic purposes, and are even taken internally. It is difficult to believe that people characterized by an anal fixation could do this. Berkeley-Hill does not mention cowdung" (Spratt 1966:209). Actually, Berkeley-Hill does mention cowdung (1921:325). Spratt's view is that "the early upbringing of Hindu children is extremely easy-going. There is very little evidence of coercion or threatening in regard to control of the bowels and bladder. The outcome of such an upbringing will be not an anal fixation but something which can be regarded as the reverse. The repression of the infant's liking for faeces, urine, and flatus will be late and weak; there will be less dislike of them than in the occidental, whose upbringing is more coercive" (Spratt 1966:210). Spratt is partly correct as we shall see later when we take up the subject of toilet training.

So Spratt, despite an avowed psychoanalytic bias, tends to dismiss the possible significance of so-called anal character. Says Spratt, ". . . it is questionable whether the Hindus' dislike of faecal contamination is any more intense than that of other people" (Spratt 1966:146). (The pertinent question here might be: How many peoples in the world employ any form of untouchability even vaguely analogous to that found in India?) Instead, Spratt favored what might properly be considered a genital explanation of the Hindu pollution complex, specifically the notion or rather fear of semen-loss. "The suggestion is, therefore, that the Hindu pollution complex which appears to underlly most of the caste rules, and to centre about saliva, is concerned at the unconscious level with semen" (Spratt 1966:150). Spratt is quite right in seeing an equivalence between saliva and semen—we have it also in the West as in the term *spitten image* to refer to a male infant who looks physically like his father (the spit being an upward displacement of semen or sperm), but Spratt fails to see that saliva is like faeces in being a body emission, a leftover which is by definition defiling.

The concept of semen-loss (cf. Edwards 1983) is also a factor in Hindu worldview. In Uttar Pradesh in northern India, it is believed (Minturn and Hitchcock 1966:74) that excessive sexual activity may cause minor illness and that "sexual intercourse is thought to make men in particular weak and susceptible to disease because the loss of one drop of semen is considered the equivalent of the loss of 40 drops of blood." Semen-loss is by no means mutually exclusive with some form of anal-character. But Spratt is perfectly clear in his repudiation of the possible anal origins of the pollution complex. "Berkeley-Hill lays great stress on the Hindu pollution complex, which is certainly a reality, but . . . it centres upon the saliva and the semen rather than the faeces" (Spratt 1966:209).

What both Berkeley-Hill and Spratt failed to understand is that they are relying too heavily on the particular description of anal erotic character described by Freud, Abraham, Jones and others, which was based upon toilet-training procedures found *in Europe*. This is a mistake also made by anthropologists as we shall soon see. The fact that the Indian situation does not conform exactly to the anal erotic portrait delineated by Freud and his followers does not a priori rule out an anal erotic infantile influence. Even Berkeley-Hill to his credit did notice that the original Freudian characterology did not apply in all respects to India. After initially claiming that the character trait of parsimony and stinginess is found among the Hindus (1920:329), he later observed that "the opposite of parsimony—extreme generosity and extravagance" is also found (1921:331).

Most Indologists and anthropologists tend to speak of pollution or impurity as the underlying impetus for caste untouchability, but they utterly fail to explain the 'origin' of pollution or impurity. I would say that calling the origin of untouchability a concept of pollution borders on tautology. If pollution makes someone or something untouchable, what is it that makes someone or something polluting? The few Indologists or anthropologists who mention the Freudian anal erotic character hypothesis typically reject it. Mary Douglas's position is representative:

> That the sociological approach to caste pollution is much more convincing than a psychoanalytic approach is clear when we consider what the Indian's private attitudes to defecation are. In the ritual we know that to touch excrement is to be defiled and that the latrine cleaners stand in the lowest grade of the caste hierarchy. If this pollution rule expressed individual anxieties we would expect Hindus to be controlled and secretive about the act of defecation. It comes as a considerable shock to read that slack disregard is their normal attitude, to such an extent that pavements, verandahs and public places are littered with faeces until the sweeper comes along. (1970:148-149)

Vatuk echoes this reasoning: "Yet there is in this society no stress on an early or strict toilet training such as might be thought to create a tendency to obsessive ritual cleanliness or, on the other hand, to an exaggerated pleasure in the verbal manipulation of feces" (1970:275).

Douglas totally misunderstood the Freudian argument. She wrongly assumed that the situation in India is analogous to the West where relatively strict toilet training of infants results in sublimation and repression of the subject of feces. The Freudian position is rather that infantile conditioning (with respect to weaning, toilet training, etc.) may be reflected in corresponding adult behavioral patterns. Thus, for example, more relaxed toilet training for Indian infants might account for Indian adults' defecating in public without shame. Douglas's own bias is revealed in her definition of "dirt." "As we know it, dirt is essential disorder. Dirt offends against order. Eliminating it is not a negative movement, but a positive effort to organize the environment" (1970:12). One wonders if Douglas were at all conscious of her word choice in saying that "eliminating" dirt is not a negative "movement," which would seem to make the act of defecation a positive one, indeed! Of course, as any Freudian can readily see, the relationship between defecation habits and order is precisely the point. Parents who insist that their infants be "regular" in their bowel habits are insisting upon orderliness.

Perhaps the clearest articulation of the relationship of dirt to caste hierarchy was made by a sociologist, not an anthropologist. Milner well understood that "In traditional India dirt is primarily social rather than physical" (1987:60). He also utilized the principle of "limited good" (Foster 1965) though without using that terminology—he refers to cleanliness purity being "an inexpansible resource" (1987:64), meaning "if some are to be clean and pure, others must remain polluted. . . .The purity of upper caste was in large measure dependent upon having lower castes responsible for the removal of waste and dirt. . . . The key point is that in the traditional concepts of Hinduism, for some caste to be clean and ritually pure, others must be dirty." This statement is strikingly similar to Dumont's view: "It is clear that the impurity of the Untouchable is conceptually inseparable from the purity of the Brahman" (1980:54). Milner also drew attention to the opposition between the kitchen and toilet areas, an opposition we noted earlier in our tales of crow and sparrow. "Purest of all is the kitchen area. . . . At the opposite extreme are the toilet facilities" (1987:65).

Milner expanded further on the impurity of the toilet in Indian culture:

> Areas that are associated with human excrement are for the orthodox Hindu inherently polluting. No matter how scientifically sanitary a toilet might be, to enter such a facility—and certainly to use it—lowers one's purity. Purity can be fully restored only by a complete bath and a clean set of clothes. . . . Moreover for the orthodox upper caste someone else must clean it; their purity can be maintained only if such work is carried out by others who absorb the pollution that is inherent in the task. Since cleaning of toilet facilities is considered inherently degrading, it is left to the lowest and most deprived strata of society. (1987:66)

Milner also distinguished between private and public areas. "If cleanliness involves primarily the redistribution of dirt rather than its elimination, it is not surprising that many of the efforts at cleaning involve moving dirt from private to public areas. . . . The merchant may keep his shop neat, orderly, and clean but do this by having the dirt and trash swept out onto the street" (1987:67). The public-private distinction is not without merit. As one observer noted, "In the West, men and women eat and drink publicly but ease themselves privately. In India it is the reverse" (Malkani 1965:112). However, I am tempted to rephrase the distinction by pointing out that the critical dichotomy is often not so much one of private versus public as it is of "inside" versus "outside." Inside is clean; outside is dirty. This paradigmatic polarity affords an additional comparison between the West and India. In German culture, for example, it is the exact opposite; that is, clean exterior versus dirty interior (Dundes 1984:103-105) as indicated in the popular expression "Aussen hui! Innen pfui". The Indian dichotomy is equally applicable to spatial relations. Space, like the body, can be divided into inside and outside. Specifically, in the Indian context, it is critical to avoid contamination from any "dirt" from outside in order to prevent defiling the "clean" inside.

As accurate as Milner's description of "dirt" in India is, he gives no explanation whatsoever for the origin of this dirt or pollution complex. He makes no reference to toilet training, for instance, nor does he discuss untouchability in particular.

Milner's emphasis on human excrement as the ultimate pollutant in India is praiseworthy, but it is by no means an original insight. "Two potent sources of impurity emanate from, or are related to, the body; one arises from bodily wastes and emissions and the other from death. . . .

But the most potent of the impurities emanate from the body itself, its emissions and wastes. And human beings whose traditional occupation it is to remove nightsoil are categorized the lowest" (Srinivas 1984:161,162). "Pollution arising from defecation affects the human body and many objects—the former only temporarily but some of the latter permanently, depending on the nature and length of their association with excreta. That is why one gets away from such pollution by scrubbing one's hands with earth or ash and washing them with water or by taking a bath but the sweeper who deals with human excreta on a professional level gets polluted permanently" (Saraf 1971:20). "All forms of excretion—barring that of the cow—are polluting, particularly defecation and menstruation. Even the most ritually pure are polluted and therefore become Untouchable between defecation and ritual purification, as distinct from merely cleaning themselves" (Zinkin 1962:14). "Substances which render things unclean are those that come out of the body, namely faeces and saliva. A bath should follow defecation (however clean the toilet) but it can be avoided by changing into a towel beforehand, the point is any garment on the body during defecation will be rendered unclean by the act" (Chakraborty and Banerji 1975:213). This latter statement beautifully exemplifies the idea of negative contagious magic! Finally, we have a short statement from analyst Carstairs: "Any secretion from inside of the body is defiling, but the most defiling of all is human excrement" (1957:81).

Despite the existence of these and similar statements in the vast ethnographic literature on India, anthropologists have gotten no closer to the underlying logic of caste and untouchability than indicating that it is something to do with concepts of "pure" and "impure"! And where do these anthropologists think concepts of pure and impure come from? That question is simply finessed (Bean 1981).

As late as 1990, we have an attempt to deny the primacy of feces as the basis of the pollution complex in India. Instead, it is "death," which is said to be "the most potent of all the sources of impurity and inauspiciousness in the life of a Hindu" (Randeria 1990:35; cf. Nagendra 1965:272). According to this argument, "The extreme pollution of the Bhangi is not due to his work as a scavenger and remover of night soil, as is usually thought to be the case. It is his association with human death in his role as cremation-ground attendant that relegates him to the very bottom of the caste hierarchy" (1990:40). The idea that it is death and not feces which underlies the concept of pollution was stated by

Dumont much earlier. His statement was made as part of a comment on a paper by psychological anthropologist George De Vos that was concerned with the psychology of pollution (1967). De Vos's principal expertise had to do with Japanese culture—he confessed he was "ignorant of the history of caste in India" (Rueck and Knight 1967:321). However, he did mention the possible connection between feelings of revulsion toward "dirt" and toilet training (1967:301). Dumont's criticism was that "India was not at all central to his discussion. For instance, he laid great emphasis on excretion, while the main source of pollution in the caste society is after all death" (Rueck and Knight 1967:317).

What Randeria, Dumont and others fail to understand is that death is symbolically equivalent to feces. In this context, it may be significant that the Hindu ideal includes the "notion of dying outside one's house, on the banks of a holy river" (Kaushik 1976:283). One is obliged to go "outside one's house" to defecate and preferably to the banks of a stream or river. But there is stronger data to support the ideas of the symbolic equivalence of untouchability and death (and feces). Just as the untouchable was supposed to drag thorns, a leaf branch, or a broom behind him to obliterate his potentially defiling footprints, so a passage in the *Rig Veda* (5:19:12) refers to a funeral practice in which mention is made of a plant that "wipes away the track (of death) which they fasten to the dead" (Brown 1957:45). The untouchable, like a corpse, is polluting or defiling. The symbolic equivalence is attested by the act that the very same technique is utilized to "wipe away" (!) the track.

As death is the end product of life, so feces is the literal end product of food. Touching feces and touching death may well be equivalent, but the crucial question with respect to Randeria's thesis is: which is primary and which is secondary? All the evidence presented in this essay tends to indicate that it is feces that is primary and death secondary. Randeria's proposal that death is the first cause of pollution is roughly analogous to Spratt's suggestion that semen-loss or saliva, not feces, was the principal factor leading to the pollution complex.

Carstairs had the right idea when he said "Beneath the concern about defilement lay a preoccupation with the noxious properties of human faeces, the arch-contaminant, which was associated with personal and social degradation" (1957:107). Novelist Naipaul put it another way when he spoke of the "blight of caste," including not only untouchability but also "the deification in India of filth" (1977:187). Earlier Naipaul had suggested that "at the heart of the system [of caste] lies the degradation of the latrine-cleaner" (1964:36,85). Anand's untouchable central character explained, "They always abuse us. Because we are sweepers. Because we touch dung. They hate dung. I hate it too. . . . For them I am a sweeper, a sweeper-untouchable! They think we are mere dirt because we clean their dirt" (1986:52,79). "We in India almost identify the Bhangi with excreta and consider him as filth. I believe in the wide world there is nothing like the Hindu Bhangi. He is the unique creation of the irrational revulsion we have for excreta" (Malkani 1965:87).

The solutions for "untouchability" are either to make everyone his own scavenger, as Gandhi, in effect, proposed, or to make no one a scavenger. Gandhi's words (1964:68): "Each person should be his own sweeper." If sweepers did not actually touch feces, they would no longer be untouchables argued novelist Anand:

> When the sweepers change their profession, they will no longer remain untouchables. And they can do that soon, for the first thing we will do when we accept the machine, will be to introduce the machine which clears dung without anyone having to handle it—the flush system. Then the sweepers can be free from the stigma of untouchability and assume the dignity of status that is their right as useful members of a casteless and classless society. (Anand 1986:155)

## Toilet Training in India

It is one thing to propose an excremental origin of caste and untouchability on the basis of folktales and ethnographic data concerning defecation habits; it is quite another to suggest a linkage between caste and untouchability on the one hand with toilet training techniques on the other. Is there any evidence from India to support such a linkage? Or is it just a matter of accepting an undocumented Freudian assertion that there is such a linkage?

First of all, the ethnographic data about toilet training in India that we have indicates that the agent of such training is female, usually the mother (Narain 1964:134) but sometimes the grandmother (Bassa 1978:341).

The equation of toilet training agent (mother) with untouchable sweepers was made repeatedly by Mahatma Gandhi. In an address published in *Young India* on February 26, 1925, Gandhi said (1954b:16): "My mother was certainly a scavenger in as much as she cleaned me when I was a child. But she did not on that account become an untouchable. Why then should a Bhangi who renders similar necessary service be regarded as untouchable?" In a statement made one month earlier on January 22, 1925, Gandhi said much the same:

> Let me make my position absolutely clear. While I do hope that the institution of untouchability as it stands today has no sanction in Hinduism, Hinduism does recognize 'untouchability' in a limited sense and under certain circumstances. For instance, every time my mother handled unclean things she became untouchable for the time being and had to cleanse herself by bathing. . . . Just as we revere our mothers for the sanitary service that she renders us when we are infants, and the greater her service the greater is our reference for her, similarly, the Bhangis are entitled to our highest reverence for the sanitary service they perform for society (1954b:22-23).

Here we have stated in the clearest possible way the equation of toilet-training mothers with sweepers. No less explicit is Bengali poet Satyendranath Datta's "Scavenger," translated by Rabindranath Tagore (1861-1941), one of India's greatest poets (1925:148):

*The Cleanser*

Why do they shun your touch, my friend,
     and call you unclean
Whom cleanliness follows at every step,
     making the earth and air sweet for our dwelling,
     and ever luring us back from return to the wild?
You help us, like a mother her child, into freshness,
     and uphold the truth, that disgust is never for man.
The holy stream of your ministry carries pollutions away
     and ever remains pure.
Once Lord Shiva had saved the world from a deluge of poison
     by taking it himself,
And you save it everyday from filth with the same divine sufferance.

Come friend, come my hero, give us courage to serve man, even while
bearing the brand of infamy from him.

The mother-sweeper equation in the context of toilet training
ritual provides a potential insight into sin-removal techniques in
adulthood. In a monograph devoted to the Hindu concept of *moksa,*
which may be roughly translated as a state of being resembling salvation,
we are told, "there is no distinction made between deliverance from sin,
from uncleanness, and from curse. Sin is uncleanness, and uncleanness
is something that man commits" (Rodhe 1946;150, 26 n.25). What is
fascinating but in a way predictable from a Freudian perspective is that
"The verb used for the *wiping off* of sins . . . is *apa-mrjate*" (Rodhe
1946:150, my italics). Eggeling in his edition of the *Satapatha-Brahmana*
(1900:266 n.1) provides an additional example when he quotes a formula
"with the help of the gods have I wiped out the sin committed against the
gods." For one thing, the use of the verb *wipe* in connection with sin is
surely suggestive. From this writer's perspective, if sin truly is equated
to uncleanness (read feces), then wiping away sin is a perfectly
appropriate metaphor. For another, the formula suggests that the god
(read parents) must help the individual wipe out the sin committed
against the gods, that is, remove the feces committed so to speak against
the parents.

A prayer to water is reportedly part of a Brahman's religious
exercises upon awakening:

> Water of the sea, of the rivers, of tanks, of wells, and
> of any other place whatsoever, hear favorably my prayers and
> vows. . . . O Water! you are the eye of sacrifice and battle!
> You have an agreeable flavour; you have the bowels of a
> mother for us, and all her feelings towards us! I call upon you
> with the same confidence with which a child at the approach
> of danger flies to the arms of a loving mother. Cleanse me
> from my sins and all other men of their sins. (Dubois
> 1906:251)

As a mother wipes feces from her infant, so deities, evidently with the
help of water and its maternal bowels, can cleanse sins away.

The point is that the mother-sweeper equation exists independent
of Freud. It may well be an inaccurate or false equation, but it is surely
noteworthy that it was articulated not by a Freudian westerner, but by

Gandhi and Tagore, two of India's greatest minds of the twentieth century. With that established, let us turn to what is known about the specifics of toilet training in India.

Generally speaking, "Almost all students of Indian personality have been struck by the extreme indulgence of the Indian child. . . ." (Kothari 1970:268), a statement made without referring specifically to toilet training. With respect to toilet training, there is widespread agreement that it is lax or relaxed. Here are some random ethnographic samples: In the rural Punjab, an observer noted: "the village child is never taught to control itself in any way. Until it is of an age to observe the ways of its elders, it behaves like an untrained dog. . . . Children are allowed to relieve themselves how and when they please. . . . A twice or thrice folded cloth is placed under a babe at night and stains are washed away in the morning, but the cloth will not be changed for 10 or 15 days" (Darling 1934:70, 188, 283). Lois Barclay Murphy, wife of psychologist Gardner Murphy, studied child development in India. She observed:

> There is little systematic toilet training; few children are forced; they seldom receive bewildering punishments for something their bodies needed to do. When small children are old enough to observe and learn where to go by watching adults, they do as older people do. Until that time, they may be treated much as we would treat a young kitten not yet old enough to train. (Murphy 1953:49)

In rural villages, "The infants and young children are nude or semi-nude (lower half nude to save soiling) and there is a complete absence of toilet training; a child can ease himself anywhere and at any time, and all that is done is that the mother comes and cleans up (in most places there are no lavatories for the adults, and they use the fields behind the bushes)" (Gupta 1956:506). Minturn and Hitchcock described toilet training in Khalapur: "Although the women sometimes show mild disgust at a baby's bowel movement, their reaction is surprisingly mild considering the extreme disgust attached to adult feces, which can be removed only by a sweeper, the lowliest of the Untouchable castes in the village" (1966:109; cf. Narain 1964:137).

Indian psychiatrists have made similar observations (though without relating these observations to the topics of caste and untouchability). According to psychiatrist Medard Boss (1965:68):

Indian pot training in early infancy is usually much more lenient than in the West. I got to know many mothers, including those of the upper classes, who allowed their two-, three-year-old offspring to crawl about on the costliest rugs and did not make the slightest fuss when what we are accustomed to referring to as "an accident" happened. Without one word of blame, the mothers would patiently and serenely clean up the little puddles of urine or the tiny piles of feces. . . . The infant is the omnipotent tyrant; his mother his obedient and devoted servant.

Sudhir Kakar, India's most prominent psychoanalyst and author of *The Inner World: A Psycho-analytic Study of Childhood and Society in India*, first published in 1978 and the most important psychoanalytic treatment of Indian personality since Carstairs' *The Twice-Born* appeared in 1957, confirms Boss's account: ". . . with respect to elimination, the toddler in India is exempt from anxious pressure to learn to control his bowel movements according to a rigid schedule of time and place. Soiling of clothes or floor is accepted in a matter of fact way and cleaned up afterwards by the mother or other older girls or women in the family without shame or disgust" (1981:103).

Some of the descriptions of toilet training in India give excellent details, especially about the chronological development of the process. Here is one of the better ethnographic depictions:

Parents do not show signs of over-anxious concern for babies to be clean and dry. In this sphere genial tolerance and permissiveness prevail; toilet training is extremely easy-going and no fuss attends the process; babies and young children are never scolded if they make a mess. Up till the age of two or more the child performs its toilet function when and where it pleases, without any scolding from the mother, who wipes up after it. After about two and a half the child is taught to go out in the yard and only at about the age of five is it expected to start using the lavatory or visit the fields with a pot of water. Up till that age the mother or some other woman washes it herself with water. There are very strict rules of faecal pollution in the Hindu system; these are only gradually instilled into the growing child, and not until it is between two and three years old. It is significant that these instructions go hand in hand with warnings about the pollution which the touch of the low castes causes, although this tabu is on the decline in cities. (Lannoy 1971:94)

It is of interest that the age of five is often singled out as the age by which a child is supposed to be fully toilet trained. "Punjabi child-rearing methods result in the child being allowed to remain in a relatively extended infancy. Punjabi mothers are highly indulgent and effectively no discipline is imposed upon the child; there is no formal toilet training and a mother will continue to wash her child after defecation at least until he is five years old" (Hershman 1974:274-275). "By the age of five or six the child has mastered the technique of bowel elimination, including proper form, the use of the left hand, etc." (Narain 1964:138). Again from Khalapur:

The last stage of this [toilet training] learning process is learning to use water to wash after a bowel movement. Mothers do this for babies and young children. By the age of 4 or 5, the children have learned to do this themselves and may sometimes be seen eliminating by a stream and washing themselves. The adult attitudes about human feces and their association with the Untouchable castes are undoubtedly communicated to the child, but no direct punishment of accidents was observed. The training seems to present no real problems for adults or children. (Minturn and Hitchcock 1966:116-117)

Kurtz's summary of Indian toilet training is helpful:

All observers seem to agree that Hindus neither praise children for exercising proper toilet habits nor do they blame or punish them for mistakes. . . . Hindu children may be "trained" or more often "train themselves" anytime between the first and the fourth or fifth years. . . . While such self-training is generally accomplished in the second, third or fourth year, a child continues to rely on others to be cleansed with water afterwards until the age of four or five. (1992:84,85)

Gandhi's comment on lenient childrearing in India: "We labour under a sort of superstition that the child has nothing to learn during the first five years of its life" (1954a:251). A report from the 1880s confirms this. A Hindu boy "usually runs about for three or four years *in puris naturalibus*. . . . When he attains the age of five, the period fixed by his parents for beginning his education, he is sent to a . . . vernacular school" (Vasu 1883:30,35). Whether this is an accurate stereotype of child development or whether this is simply another illustration of the influence of the ritual number five in India cannot be determined.

From the consistent picture of toilet training in India thus far, can we see any parallels or repercussions in adult behavior? Certainly the apparent laissez-faire attitude that permits a toddler to ease him or herself where and when he wishes is not the least incompatible with the adult technique of going to different places outside the home, seemingly indiscriminately. Indeed, the adult practice would seem to be directly parallel to the common infantile experience.

It is tempting to speculate about a possible correlation between toilet training and attitudes toward time. The Germans, for example, start toilet training early with infants around five months old, and hope that a child is completely "housebroken" by the time it is a year old (Dundes 1984:89). The Germans are famous for being punctual as part of their concern for orderliness. In contrast, Indian infants are not expected to be "housebroken" until much later, e.g., the age of five. One of the alleged characteristics of general Indian personality is a "lack of time-sense" (Dave 1991:91). Flexibility with respect to time as signaled by the sarcastic expression, "Indian Standard Time," and as articulated by such views "that normally, Indians do not get upset if things do not happen in time or according to schedule" (Dave 1991:91) could conceivably be related to the relatively long and relaxed period of toilet training (Muensterberger 1969:204).

Perhaps less speculative and more explicit as an apparent 'result' of the particulars of Indian toilet training are some ethnographic details seemingly related to the cleansing of the infant/child by the mother or mother surrogate. Keeping in mind that a man's wife is, in the Freudian view, a substitute for the man's mother (in the same way as a wife's husband is supposed to be a substitute for her father), we may consider the following curious incidents. In one report (Darling 1934:188) a boy in a village "fouled his bed after his bride came to live with him, and when they heard of it, the village laughed." The observer in this instance actually related the incident to the fact that Punjabis "are allowed to relieve themselves how and when they please." He failed, however, to see an Oedipal aspect of the event. But an even more striking example is reported from Mysore by Dubois although the data was considered so bizarre as to require Dubois to write an editorial disclaimer as a cautionary preamble: "There are, nevertheless, some customs which, although scrupulously observed in the countries where they exist, are so strongly opposed to the rules of decency and decorum generally laid down that they are spoken of with disapprobation and sometimes with horror by the rest of the community." The following may be mentioned among practices of this nature.

"In the interior of Mysore, women are obliged to accompany the male inmates of the house whenever the latter retire for the calls of nature, and to cleanse them with water afterwards. This practice, which is naturally viewed with disgust in other parts of the country, is here regarded as a sign of good breeding and is most carefully observed" (1906:18-19). Fortunately, we have another report that corroborates Dubois' account: "In Tanjore, I have been told, there is one particular Brahman subcaste which is so particular about the polluting effect of defecation that the wife has to pour water over her husband to clean him. He does not have to touch himself, so he is spared the rigorous full purification and can make do with reciting a few mantras and sprinkling some water on his head" (Zinkin 1962:15). Even a non-Freudian ought to be able to perceive an infantile origin of such adult behavior. The adult male has his wife cleanse him after defecation just as his mother did in his infancy. The infantile pleasure enjoyed during years of maternal cleansing rituals is achieved into adulthood with the wife taking the mother's role. From a Freudian perspective, this practice is not at all unexpected or strange. In the same way, the Punjabi boy who fouled his bed after his bride came to live with him could reflect the same sort of pattern. Defecating in bed in front of one's wife would be a direct continuation of defecating in bed in front of one's mother.

We are now better able to understand the seemingly strange custom of taking a bath and changing clothes after coming inside from the outside, e.g., after coming home from school. This would seem to be irrational behavior but once one realizes that untouchables are "feces," then contact with untouchables requires the same sort of purification procedure that an infant/child undergoes. When a toddler comes in after defecating outside, he is washed and perhaps given new clothes!

## The Crackdown Paradox

Thus far we have been able to detect some parallels between toilet training in India and adult defecation habits, but a troubling question remains. If Indian toilet training is really so lenient and relaxed, why is there almost an obsessive concern with cleanliness, purity, defilement, etc? How can lenient toilet training "cause" a belief in "untouchability?" The short answer is: it cannot.

It is my contention that the "leniency" described so often and so fully for Indian infants and children is somewhat misleading. Yes, by western standards, the toilet training is surely lenient and gentle and undemanding. But I believe the infant is given a mixed message. The leniency is offset by two important factors. First is the extremely *early* initiation of toilet training albeit lenient training, and second a devastating "crackdown" at or about age five when the pollution complex boom is lowered on a previously indulged child. It is this mixed message, so to speak, that I believe may be largely responsible for the continuation of the pollution complex and untouchability.

Let us discuss these two factors in some depth. In an acclaimed cross-cultural study of the possible relationships between child training generally and adult personality, Whiting and Child reported (1953:74): "The median estimate for the beginning age of serious toilet training falls at the age of two. Slightly over half of the primitive societies (14 out of 25) began toilet training somewhere between the ages of one and a half and two and a half." The range ran essentially from six months to five years. In that context, we can see that, in German cultures, the custom of beginning toilet training at the age of 5 months is very much at the early end of the spectrum (Dundes 1984:89-90). What about India? One survey of child-rearing practices in India mentioned several different reports to the effect that "toilet training starts as early as at three months" (Jaiswal and Grewal 1988:32, 37). Bassa claimed (1978:341), on the basis of twenty years experience in a Bombay community health center with more than 100 children studied, that traditional toilet training is "introduced early by grandmother at 3-4 months." These statistics surely seem to be counter to the claim that in the Hindu family, there are "no premature efforts to force regular and cleanly habits regarding urination and defecation" (Banerjee 1944-1945:184). To be sure, the Indic situation is unlike Germany where toilet training is both early and strict. In India, in contrast, the toilet training is early but lenient. The paradox, if there is a paradox, would be that parents, or the mother in this instance, is sending two different conflicting messages. Early initiation of training, e.g., at three months, would hint at a parental wish for the child to control and direct this activity while the parental (mostly maternal) willingness to wait until the child is three years old or more to complete toilet training would convey to the child that he or she is relatively free from societal pressure in this area. One theory is that mothers may intentionally prolong the period of infancy for their own purposes and pleasure (Marfatia 1943-1944:303; cf. Sinha 1977:97). Mothers as women feeling subjugated by men might presumably enjoy the feeling of power and control over (male) infants (cf. Slater 1968).

While there are so many diverse populations in India making it difficult to generalize—"No generalizations are possible with regard to child rearing practices in India" (Jaiswal and Grewal 1988:38)—we do find repeated indications that "There was little systematic toilet training" (1988:31, 32, 34, 38). Similarly, in Sri Lanka, elimination training was said to be "mild" (Straus 1957:27). The discrepancy between early initiation of toilet training and lenient toilet training does not really become traumatic until what has been termed the *crackdown* occurs. To understand the significance of the *crackdown*, it is necessary to consider the notion of cultural discontinuities.

Perhaps the first major articulation of the concept of cultural discontinuities was by anthropologist Ruth Benedict in a brilliant but neglected essay entitled "Continuities and Discontinuities in Cultural Conditioning," which appeared in *Psychiatry* in 1938. In that essay, Benedict delineated what she called discontinuities in western culture with special emphasis on differentiating infant-child conditioning from adult behavioral norms. She discussed three distinct areas or axes: responsible versus nonresponsible roles, dominance-submission, and adult behavioral and attitudinal norms of sexuality. Her main point was that American infants/children are initially taught to be nonresponsible—in contrast to adult expectations of responsibility, to be submissive (to parents/elders)—in contrast to exercising dominance as an adult, and being taught to consider sexuality as a forbidden or sinful activity—in contrast to adult acceptance of and participation in sexuality. From Benedict's perspective, Americans have to learn, or rather *un*learn "rules" imposed during early childhood in order to accept responsibility for one's actions, to be dominant (e.g., in being a leader), and to be able to engage in sexual activity without feelings of guilt. Benedict's insights seem valid to me. If an American child is told that sexuality is "dirty" or "sinful," right up until the time that child is about to be married, then it may be difficult, if not impossible, for that child when it becomes an adult to undo that cultural conditioning. Can the religious (or secular) ritual of a wedding accomplish that undoing? Does the new status of "marriage" suddenly alter years of treating sexuality as something brutish and animalistic? Presumably new trends in sex education since the appearance of Benedict's essay may have helped mitigate the disastrous effects of this serious cultural discontinuity.

Benedict also suggested that some nonwestern societies demonstrate much more continuity between child and adult norms. Thus, a little boy may "practice" techniques later used to hone hunting skills or a little girl may "practice" techniques anticipating later domestic chores. On the other hand, Benedict also noted: "Many primitive societies expect as different behavior from an individual as a child and as an adult as we do, and such discontinuity involves a presumption of strain" (1938:165). It is this notion of cultural discontinuity that I suspect may be at the very heart of untouchability, inasmuch as Indian toilet training (as well as Indian child-rearing generally) is marked by a decisive and abrupt total shift in attitudinal and behavioral expectations.

It has long been recognized that ". . . the constant nursing during childhood and the late, and relatively easy weaning . . . develops the acute sense of dependence" (Taylor 1948:11) in Indian children. Kothari, speaking about childhood socialization in general and not about toilet training in particular, suggested that "Extreme indulgence of the child whose very cry for pleasure and relief is agreeably solicited by the mother results in patterns of dependence and dominance that persist into adulthood. . . . When the individual grows up the pattern persists in the form of superior-subordinate relationships, conformity with formal rules and rituals, and a keen sensitivity to hierarchies of age and status" (1970:272). That would appear to be a description of continuities, not discontinuities. But the same author also observed that "the long and intense period of maternal indulgence" is followed by "a sudden withdrawal after this period" and furthermore that "the experience of over-indulgence followed by sudden deprivation produces opposite strains in the personality . . . marked optimism—often unrealistic . . . and insecurity [which] may lead to bouts of depression arising from a pervasive concern with the self and its effectiveness" (Kothari 1970:273).

Another comment along the same lines argued that prolonged

breastfeeding and the lack of strict toilet training during the period of Hindu childhood "may promote early security but later, a feeling of helplessness (or passivity) in adult life seems to prevail" (Gandhi 1974:59-60). The writer continues, "It is this fixation on the early modes of gratification which has also been held to be a contributive factor a strong identification with the mother and the consequent needs for submission to authority. . . ." (Gandhi 1974:60).

Among the several observers who have remarked on the abruptness of the dramatic change in parent-infant relations, it was psychoanalyst Carstairs who was one of the first to articulate it: "I suggest that this relatively late reversal of a previously dominating (although emotionally inconsistent) relationship with his mother has a profound effect upon the child's later development. . . . It is as if he were accustomed again and again to climb a certain step and then suddenly found the step no longer there. His confidence is shattered. . . ." (1957:158). This statement of Carstairs—which actually refers to weaning, not toilet training, has been criticized (cf. Moudgil 1972:126) on the grounds that social or historical factors can explain Hindu personality better than Carstairs' "rather rigid neo-Freudianism" (1972:131).

Carstairs' insight is confirmed by psychiatrist Medard Boss, according to whom: "The greatest damage inflicted by Indian methods of upbringing on mental health . . . is because the children hardly turned four, five, or six, have abruptly imposed on them a very brusque withdrawal by their parents, a vehement insistence on the most meticulous cleanliness" (1965:72). As soon as they can understand, "the children have impressed on them energetically the idea that the morning bowel movement and the bath are the two most important events of the day" (1965:73). This reminds us of Carstairs' remark: "Every informant who was asked to describe the happenings of a day in his life began by mentioning his going to stool, and then his bathing, as being two of the most significant events of the day" (1957:81). Feces and the removal thereof through bathing are thus features that correspond to the adult obsession with "pollution" and "purity." Boss argued that Indian children experience a very free, permissive atmosphere during the first years of their lives and "were compelled only relatively late, at the age of three, five or six, to experience an abrupt prohibition of their animality" (1965:81). The key word here is "abrupt".

In an important essay on childrearing in India, D. M. Bassa

referred to the cultural discontinuity or crackdown as "a *cardinal crisis*" (1978:342, his italics). Bassa also claimed that "The early toilet training conduces to a severe superego and obsessional trends" (1978:342). It may be Roland who should be credited with coining *crackdown*. "Various commentators on Indian childhood all testify to a severe and often sudden crackdown on the child, usually starting between the ages of 3 to 5 or 6 and lasting through the latency years well into adolescence" (Roland 1980:78). Roland also echoed Bassa's statement "This crackdown, lasting well through the latency years, results in . . . a severe latency superego" (1980:79). Roland later noted that the crackdown on behavior at age five or six in Indian child-rearing is "something not at all present in Western child-rearing" (1982:235, n.9).

Indian psychoanalyst Kakar corroborated the occurrence of the crackdown, calling it instead "The Second Birth" (1981:125, 156). The term of reference may vary, but what is described is surely recognizable. Rajan (1957:43, 44) labeled it the "age of accountability." Kakar first calls attention to the "period of prolonged infancy" enjoyed by the Indian child (1981:80) such that the period of infancy "extends through the first four or five years of life" and consequently "it is not until between the ages of three and five that an Indian child moves away (in a psychological sense) from the first all-important 'Other' in his life, his mother" (1981:79, 80). Speaking specifically of what he labels "The Second Birth," Kakar noted, ". . . for the male child especially, the abruptness of the separation from his mother and the virtual reversal of everything that is expected of him may have traumatic developmental consequences. . . . Even more than the suddenness of the transition, the *contrast* between an earlier, more or less unchecked benevolent indulgence and the new inflexible standards of absolute obedience and conformity to familial and social standards is its striking feature" (1981:126-127).

Not everyone accepts the notion of a crackdown phase in Indian childhood. Kurtz, for example, in his stimulating book *All the Mothers Are One: Hindu India and the Cultural Reshaping of Psychoanalysis* rejected the notion. First he cites Indian anthropologist Dube's account of toilet training in his 1955 *Indian Village*. According to Dube, "Toilet training . . . is completely neglected, and soiling of clothes does not arouse any disgust" (1955:192). After a child learns to walk, there are attempts at toilet training. "When the child wakes up in the morning the mother seats it on the hollow made by joining her feet and keeps on

making a hissing sound which is believed to induce a child to ease itself
. . . . If the child wets or soils its clothes at this stage the mother or a
sibling will say, '*Chhi*, you are dirty.' But this is done with a smile and
there is hardly any reproach in the remark" (1955:193). Then Dube con-
cludes, "Later childhood begins at about five. . . . Toilet training
becomes strict, and the child is expected to have full control over
defecation and urination. Cleanliness is insisted upon, and any failure on
his part in this respect arouses anger in the elders. The erring child is
ridiculed, chastised and punished" (1955:194). Kurtz (1992:89) calls this
last statement by Dube "a classic description of the so-called crackdown
phase that follows the early 'indulgence' of Hindu infants." But Kurtz
does not accept this "so-called crackdown at age five) and feels that the
conditioning is gradual and that it has been "misinterpreted as a
dangerously traumatic imposition on a pampered and unprepared child"
(1992:89).

Kurtz offered the term *renunciation* (1992:9, 55-89) as an
alternative to what occurs at age five. Kurtz maintained that Indian child
rearing is simply different from western child rearing such that the Indian
child participates in an unforced, noncoercive voluntary "renunciation"
of the maternal breast, interest in fecal materials, and other pleasurable
activities "in return for membership in the group" (1992:9, 61, 101,
122). Kurtz is primarily concerned with weaning and the development of
a multiple maternal image rather than with toilet training (but see
1992:84-85). In any event, he is skeptical about the abrupt reversal
theory championed by Carstairs, Kakar and others. He claimed that "the
traditional psychoanalytic picture of excessive early indulgence followed
by a late, abrupt withdrawal of pleasure is too simple" (1992:75). Kurtz,
however, offered no real ethnographic evidence to refute the numerous
descriptions of the "crackdown" phase, and the reader should keep in
mind that these descriptions were made by Indian anthropologists and
psychoanalysts. Moreover, despite Kurtz's adamant allegiance to
psychoanalytic theory, his proposal that "group membership" should take
precedence over "id" pleasure principle activities smacks of the old-
fashioned social anthropological bias that inevitably insists on placing
social organizational concerns above all other determinants in culture.
Kurtz's usage of the epithet "so-called" in connection with the crackdown phase seems inappropriate in the light of considerable ethnographic
reportage attesting to the existence of such a phase.

It would seem to me that Benedict's notion of cultural

discontinuity is very much applicable to Indian child-rearing techniques. The trauma arising from such a marked discontinuity could well result in a cathexis or fixation on anality. The combination of early toilet training (three months) with a strict enforcement of cleanliness norms at age five, which are in contrast to the generally permissive and lenient first five years of life, is very different from child-rearing patterns in the West. I believe that Spratt was very much mistaken when he said that "It is difficult to believe that people characterized by an anal fixation" could use cowdung daily and even ingest it (Spratt 1966:212). Indians do have an anal fixation, and they do on occasion ingest cowdung. But to understand this more fully, we must briefly consider the special position of the cow in Hindu culture.

## The Cow Anomaly

The sacredness of the cow in India has been discussed by many, many authors (e.g., Crooke 1912; Ram 1926-1927; Brown 1957; Roy 1958; Margul 1968; Sharma 1968; Simoons 1974, 1979; Srinivasan 1979; Lodrick 1981; and Eichinger Ferro-Luzzi 1987). Most of the anthropological literature takes an ecological approach (Harris 1965, 1978; Simoons 1979; and Nair 1987), which argues that the cow is important for its production of fuel (cowdung) and food (milk).

Several aspects of sacred cow worship in India cannot be explained fully in terms of ecology. I am thinking of the widespread practice of using cowdung as a cleansing agent—most peoples on the face of the earth would not think of cow manure as a particularly effective cleansing agent, and the even more perplexing custom of ingesting pancha-gavia, the five products of the cow in combination; milk, curds, clarified butter, urine, and dung. Both of these features of bovine veneration involve feces, which suggests that they may well be related to the general topic of this extended essay.

To better appreciate the special place the cow occupies in India, we may cite a poem chanted by unmarried girls in Bengal in connection with a spring ritual in which grass is ceremonially offered to a cow. The poem spells out the various positive traits of the cow giving due emphasis to the admirable powers of cowdung:

Of all animals the cow is the most sacred. Every part

of her body is inhabited by some deity, each hair of her body is inviolable. All her excretions are hallowed. Any spot which a cow has condescended to honour with the sacred deposit of her excrement is forever consecrated ground, and the filthiest place with it is at once cleansed and freed from pollution, while ashes produced by burning this substance are of such a holy nature that they not only make clean all material things, but have only to be sprinkled over a sinner to convert him into a saint. (Das 1953:233)

Venerating cowdung would be a curiosity in any culture, but in India with its demonstrated almost pathological fear of feces of any other kind including human, it becomes truly an anomaly. This has not escaped the notice of anthropologists, but they seem unable to do more than describe the situation. They have not, to my knowledge, offered any plausible explanation of the anomaly. Anthropologist M. N. Srinivas commented: "The cow, when alive, is holy, like the river Ganga, and both transcend the duality of pure-impure. The live cow purifies . . . even its body products constitute a powerful and versatile purifying agent, quite the opposite of the situation with regard to bodily wastes of human beings" (1984:161). Harper articulated the anomaly by raising questions: "Since the feces and urine of any animal are impure, how do we account for their use as purifying agents? Are the feces of a cow an exception to this statement? I do not think so. Cow-dung, like the dung of any other animal, is intrinsically impure and can cause defilement—in fact, it will defile a god; but it is pure relative to a mortal" (Harper 1964:182). Harper goes on to say that the cow is a "living god" and that "the cow's most impure part is sufficiently pure relative to even a Brahman priest to remove the latter's impurities" (1964:183).

Carstairs quoted one Brahman informant's free association to the word Gobar (cow-dung): "Cow-dung—dirty stuff. . . . It's bad because it's excrement, but it's good because it purifies. And it is useful as fuel, too. They give it to you to eat when you undergo a purification. Bullocks' and buffaloes', their dung doesn't purify you. . . . We call cows 'Cow-Mother', but you don't find us calling oxen or buffaloes 'father'. The Gods themselves consider the cow as sacred" (1957:323). Certainly most Westerners would find the use of cow dung to cleanse kitchen utensils (Simoons 1974:27) to be a repellent practice, but not nearly as repellent as eating the substance.

Panchagavya is the term that refers to the mixture of the five products of the cow. The reader should note that this is yet one more important illustration of the presence of the ritual number five in India (cf. Eichinger Ferro-Luzzi 1977:512-513). This mixture is believed to be a powerful purifying agent, more or less equivalent to fire or Ganges water (Simoons 1974:28). Ganges water is itself a cultural anomaly. It is defined as pure even though it is no different from any other river or stream in India. As one Indian author put it, "All Ganges water is pure and so we drain the filth of cities into it and drink it away as very pure" (Malkani 1965:22). In response to westerners' objections, informants claim: "It lies not in the power of man to pollute the Ganges" and "Filtering Ganges water takes the holiness out" (Mayo 1932:262; cf. Alley 1994). The use of Pancha-gavia is limited to situations deemed especially defiling. An outcaste desiring to be readmitted to his caste might have his tongue burned or a part of his body branded with red-hot iron (cf. the tales of crow and sparrow) and "Finally, to complete his purification, he is made to drink the pancha-gavia" (Dubois 1906:42). At a funeral, the son "sips the five products of the cow which confer ceremonial purity, i.e., milk, curds, clarified butter, urine, and cow dung (Pañcagavya), though many Brahmans nowadays substitute milk, curds, clarified butter, honey, and sugar (Pañcamrita)" (Stevenson 1920:166; cf. Simoons 1974:30). This latter mixture Hutton (1963:108) called "a degenerate concession to civilized squeamishness." Dubois also reported the use of the mixture just prior to funerals, remarking that the priest "pours a few drops of the pancha-gavia into the mouth of the dying man, by virtue of which his body becomes perfectly purified" (Dubois 1906:482). The connection of the cow with death is also signaled by the custom of bringing a cow into the room of a dying man so that he can hold the cow's tail. "It is believed that the sacred cow will lead the departing soul safely into the other world" (Fuchs 1950:195; Stevenson 1920:141; Dubois 1906:483).

The substitute for pancha-gavia which uses honey and sugar in place of urine and dung is evidently not a recent innovation. Dubois discussed it in his coverage of pancha-gavia. "I have already explained of what disgusting materials the mixture known by this name is composed. . . . There is also another lustral preparation called pancha-amrita, which is composed of milk, curds, liquefied butter, honey, and sugar mixed together. This is not filthy and disgusting like the one previously mentioned, but then it is much less efficacious" (Dubois 1906: 152-153). O'Malley confirms this point in *Indian Caste Customs*: "*Panchamrita* is said to be as efficacious as *panchgavya* for minor offences, but the latter is necessary for major offences, especially a voyage to Europe" (O'Malley 1976:75). "Many a hapless member of a traditional Brahman family has returned from three years studying law or commerce in a European university and consumed a mouthful of this vile mixture before being allowed to embrace his own parents" (Baker 1990:51).

There are many, many other facets of cow veneration in India. It is considered a serious crime to kill a cow (cf. Ram 1926-1927: 281). Cows were and are protected; they are allowed to wander and forage where they wish. For some religious exercises, "devotees had to live and sleep among cows in a cow-pen, or to follow a cow everywhere" (Ram 1927-1927:292-293). Homes for aged and infirm cattle have been established (Lodrick 1981). The question remains: Why do cows enjoy such a privileged position in India?

The answer is that the cow is regarded as a mother (Ram 1926-1927:289; Emerson 1930:110; Sharma 1968:463; Hershman 1977: 281-286; Das 1985:85), or as mother earth (Crooke 1912:303). As a young college graduate in Udaipur told a psychoanalyst visiting India, "The cow is our Mother; we should never kill her. . . . The cow, you understand, is a symbol of our mother" (Bychowski 1968:61). "It is the eating of the cow's flesh that has made some castes the most reprehensible in Hindu society. It is because the cow is a sacred animal for the Hindus, who worship it as the Gomata (mother cow)" (Hanumanthan 1979:41). This is not a new insight. "The unique veneration accorded to the cow in Hinduism seems clearly to be related to the mother fixation" (Spratt 1966:194). But no one to date seems to have used the cow-mother equation as the basis for probing the meaning of cowdung used as a cleansing agent or the symbolic significance of the Pancha-gavya.

The mother is the primary caregiver for the first five years of a child's life and that care includes functioning as the agent of toilet training. The mother or mother surrogate (e.g., grandmother) removed all the infant's emissions, including urine and feces. Moreover, she did not seem to be polluted or defiled by absorbing all of the infant's pollutants. In the Punjab, we learn of "the village woman's difficulty in keeping herself sufficiently clean to pray five times a day [again the number five]. A mother always keeps her infant with her, generally in her arms, and as the napkin [diaper] has not found its way into the village, accidents happen" (Darling 1934:70). But from the infant's eye view, the mother is initially always there to give milk and to remove body wastes. This infantile situation is projected into adult religion. There is a hymn (Sharma 1968:458) honoring the cow:

> The two great vessels, Heaven and Earth have both been filled
> By the spotted cow with the milk of but one milking,
> Pious people, drinking of it, cannot diminish it.
> It becomes neither more nor less.

Again from an infantile perspective, the maternal breast appears to be inexhaustible. The infant drinks until satisfied and then later when thirsty, the same breast magically serves to quench that thirst. And the endless bounty of the maternal cow provides much more than milk as the following Kannada nursery rhyme (Sharma 1968:460) attests:

> Living, I yield milk, butter and curd, to sustain mankind
> My dung is as fuel used,
> Also to wash floor and wall;
> Or, burnt, becomes the sacred ash on forehead.
> When dead, of my skin are sandals made,
> Or the bellows at the blacksmith's furnace;
> Of my bones are buttons made. . .
> But of what use are you, O Man?

Adults treat cows in a way consonant with how mothers treat infants. Mothers allow toddlers to defecate outside where and when they please; adults allow cows to defecate outside where and when they please. Religious devotees obliged to follow a cow everywhere is analogous to infants following a mother everywhere. As the mother is apparently not at all defiled by the infant's body products, so adults are not defiled by the cow's body products. As the infant regards his or her mother as a primary cleansing agent, so the adult regards a cow as a primary provider of a cleansing agent: cow dung. As the mother is the exception to the normal rules of pollution, so also is the cow exempt from these rules. The mother's *taking* feces from the infant is paralleled by the adult's *taking* feces from the cow. From an infantile perspective, the taking of its feces by its mother is closely associated with a feeling of cleanness. By a simple twist of infantile logic, taking the feces of the cow is believed to provide a means of producing a state of cleanliness. This belief, of course, is a cultural construction. Cow dung is neither more nor less "clean" than the feces of other animals. Some informants, in response to an anthropologist's query as to why cow dung was not "dirty," claimed that since the cow eats only grass, its feces are pure, this in contrast to other animals which being omnivorous produce "dirty" feces (Hershman 1977:284, n.20).

The cow-mother reversal is part of a larger pattern. Normally, the direction is from initial pure to impure, or to employ a digestive metaphor, from food to feces, but there are a select number of ritual reversals. Harris cited Dube (1955:84) to remind us that "the cattle roam about the shrubs and rocks and eat whatever fodder is available there." He then claimed, "The sacred cow is an exploited scavenger. . . ." (Harris 1965:223). Mayo (1932:174) reported: "I have seen the cow driven by starvation so far from her natural niceness as to become a scavenger of human excrement. The sight is common." Parry calls attention to the cow's ability to transform impurities into purificatory agents. He claimed that the cow's mouth "is commonly said to be the only impure part of its body—for it feeds on refuse, garbage and other impurities" (Parry 1985:627). Yet its excrement is valued as an agent of purification. Parry sees a parallel to the "Ganges which absorbs the city's sewerage and transforms it into holy water" (1985:624). So the cow and the Ganges can reverse the normal direction from pure to impure. Instead, the impure becomes pure. I suggest that this is clearly analogous to the infant's perception of the mother for whom normally "impure" feces is undefiling. A mother cow or a mother river in adult mythology has the same remarkable transformative powers. Ganges water may look impure, but it is culturally regarded as pure, indeed as holy water. The analogy of the purifying power of the Ganges with the maternal cleansing of a soiled infant is no mere idle conjectural speculation on my part. In Benares, an investigator specifically asked informants what happens to the Ganges after "the corpses of humans and animals, bathers' soap, and human excrement enter the river?" The informants responded that "the Ganga can never be impure," explaining "Ganga is like a mother who cleans up the messes her child makes" (Alley 1994:129). In the same way, cow dung might strike the uninitiated as being just like any other animal feces, but it is culturally regarded as a purificatory agent. This is why "A Brahman, drinking water from the vessel of a Chandala, has to undergo the penance of living on cow's urine for a number of days" (Ghurye 1961:96). All this, of course, is not physical reality but psychological reality. Yet psychological reality counts!

For those who may be skeptical about this reasoning, let me cite a most curious custom that was evidently once apart of the Brahman funeral ceremony. According to Dubois (1906:486), "Then follows a most extraordinary ceremony, which at the same time is certainly a very disgusting one, the chief mourner placing his lips successively to all the apertures of the deceased's body, addressing to each a *mantram* appropriate to it, kissing it, and dropping on it a little ghee. By this ceremony the body is supposed to be completely purified." From the present analytic perspective, all the apertures that normally exude potentially defiling substances are now sealed with a product from the cow (mother) that constitutes one last cleaning by the mother figure.

Now what about the prohibition against killing cows? Or the food taboo prohibiting the eating of beef? Can this be explained? We remind the reader that both traditionally and in modern times, "most of the care of the small child and responsibility for his welfare have fallen to the mother. . . ." (Mencher 1963:59) and that the "crackdown seems first and foremost to be instituted by the mothering person(s). . . ." (Roland 1980:78; cf. Bassa 1978:341). This betrayal, so to speak, by the mother leads to feelings of ambivalence toward the mother figure "because of the shift from secure authority to insecure abandonment" (Nandy 1980:14). Since weaning, like toilet training, is gradual and relatively late, breastfeeding lasts "well past the eruption of teeth" (Silvan 1981:94). Although Bassa claimed that among Indian infants, "Aggression is not sublimated into play," he also noted "there may be much biting and pinching of his mother's "failing" breast involving some counter-aggression from her" (1978:338). Sinha made a similar comment: "During teething time the child may apply a hard bite to the tit, inflicting pain to the mother. Some mothers are known to be sensitive to such bites and may either refuse to feed the child properly or punish it otherwise" (1977:97). Analysts have maintained, ". . . it is clinically clear for both women and men that aggression toward authority figures is simply not countenanced. . . . These strictures against aggression toward the authority figure are also profoundly internalized within the Indian conscience and can operate in a quite unconscious way where a variety of defenses may be used, including and particularly, reaction-formation" (Roland 1982:245). In his insightful comment on Roland, analyst Silvan stated ". . . the society . . . discourages expressions of oral aggression. . . . Eating the cow, the giver of milk, is rigidly forbidden . . . the impulse to bite has been forced to unconsciousness" (Silvan 1981:96). What all this means is that in the case of the "sacred" cow, we have the hatred and aggressive impulse toward the mother (and her breast) transformed by means of reaction formation into excessive love expressed toward cows (as mother figures) and a rigid refusal to bite (eat) her breast (flesh). In other words, the urge or wish to bite that the infant feels becomes, in adult terms, the tendency not to bite the breast, that is, not to eat beef. The reason why adults can ingest the products of the cow but not eat the flesh of the cow can also be understood. The infant is permitted to nurse from its mother (that is, ingest the mother's body products), but not bite the breast (that is, eat mother (cow)'s flesh.

I do not believe that food taboos can be fully explained on the basis of purely ecological or economic principles à la Marvin Harris (1965, 1978). What economic principle, for example, could provide a rationale for the ingestion of the pancha-gavya? In any case, at the very least we have offered what I hope are plausible explanations for some of the most puzzling features of cow veneration in contemporary India. As for explicit evidence of a tendency toward oral aggression directed at the breast, I remind the reader of one of the Bengali versions of the first tale of crow and sparrow (supra p.30) when the crow proposed, "Whoever of us will finish eating all the grains of the field will be the winner and the winner will eat a bit of meat from the chest of the other." If we take folktales seriously, and I certainly do, then this kind of content would appear to be relevant.

## Sati (Suttee) and the Theory of Leftovers

I should now like to consider the Indian attitude toward feces in a slightly larger context as a means of explaining untouchability. The larger context is what I call "leftovers" (cf. Malamoud 1972 and Kristeva 1982:76). The underlying premise is that all leftovers, including body emissions, food, water, etc., are impure or defiling. The connection of sweepers with feces should be well established by now in the mind of the reader, but there are other castes that are considered untouchable. For example, leather-workers and barbers are usually classified as untouchables. I would suggest that the skins of dead animals constitute "leftovers," perhaps symbolic equivalents of feces, but more of that later. So also hair from human heads would also count as leftovers, and that is why barbers who handle hair are deemed untouchable.

Let me illustrate the utility of this theory of leftovers. Fuchs, for example, understands why leather workers are untouchable because they work with the skins of dead animals, but he cannot understand why weavers should be such low status. "There is no obvious reason why weaving should be ritually impure" (Fuchs 1981:178). But there is an obvious reason. Wool is a body by-product, just like human hair. Once it has been removed from the sheep, it is a "leftover" and consequently anyone who works with such a product is automatically polluted hence untouchable.

It may be helpful in understanding the concept of leftovers to recall the "inside-outside" portion of the purity paradigm in Indic culture (cf. supra p.62). Inside is clean; outside is dirty. The hair of a human, the skin of a horse, and the wool of a sheep are all "outside" and hence dirty and polluting. Moreover when an "inside" substance, such as saliva or semen, is emitted, it is immediately transformed into an "outside" one, hence, it is dirty and polluting—even to the emitter.

Saliva may also be newly considered under the rubric of leftovers. We have already discussed why Hindus abhor the use of European toothbrushes. The fear of saliva is second only to the fear of feces. This was recognized by Dubois who suggested it as an explanation of why it was considered shameful to play on wind instruments in India:

> I suppose it is on account of the defilement which the players contract by putting such instruments to their mouths after they have once been touched by saliva, which, as I shall show presently is the one excretion from the human body for which Hindus display invincible horror. (Dubois 1906:64)

Dubois' explanation for why wind instruments are played only by barbers and pariahes (Dubois 1906:63-64) sounds reasonable enough, but it should be pointed out that there could also be an anal connection. One "rule" stated that if anyone (except a Brahman) broke wind in the presence of a superior caste, his punishment consisted of losing "his hind parts" (Kamble 1982:14). There is a lot more to be said about the role of "wind" in India. For example, we may detect an anal origin of the so-called "wind illness" found in India and in adjacent areas such as Thailand (cf. Zimmerman 1979 and Muecke, 1979). In one North Indian village, "wind" more than two other humors (bile and phlegm) was "most frequently cited by villagers as the source of illness" (Raheja 1988b:258, n.3). In Thailand, one of the most common means of being attacked by wind illness is "smelling a noxious odor" (Muecke 1979:276). Ever since Whiting and Child's pioneering *Child Training and Personality* appeared in 1953, anthropologists have been alert to recognize the possibility of finding correlations between infantile conditioning and theories of disease causation. Strict or relaxed weaning, toilet-training, etc., could be reflected in both cultural explanations of disease and the cures for those diseases. In sum, the treatment of toilet training in India could account for why "wind illness" would make sense to adult Indians and why in the Punjab, for example, people exiting from a mosque could be asked "to blow upon children that are sick." One informant claimed "to be able to cure all diseases sent by God, simply by his breath" (Darling 1934:53).

Finally, on the subject of winds, let me cite some ethnographic detail that confirms both the importance of winds in the body and the ritual number five. Dubois reported the following pre-meal ode to winds ritual evidently observed by Brahmans: "He takes a little rice soaked in melted butter and puts it into his mouth saying: 'Glory to the wind which dwells in the chest!' At the second mouthful, 'Glory to the wind which dwells in the face!' And the third, 'Glory to the wind which dwells in the throat!' At the fourth, 'Glory to the wind which dwells in the whole body!' At the fifth, 'Glory to those noisy ebullitions which escape above and below!'" (Dubois 1906:246). Dubois also referred to the five winds in relating how an old man revealed to him how in his youth he sought to become holy:

> My master told me that an infallible means for making rapid progress towards spirituality was to keep all the apertures of my body completely closed, so that none of the five *pranams* (winds) which are in it could escape. To do this I had to place a thumb in each ear, close my lips with the fourth and little fingers of each hand, my eyes with the two forefingers, and my nostrils with the two middle fingers; and to close the lower orifice I had to cross my legs and sit very tightly on one of my heels. (1906:532)

It is of interest that in both these two last rituals, the fifth and last item referred to the anus, a small hint that the bodily origin of caste discussion earlier in this essay suggesting that untouchables came from a fifth area of the body might be correct. Winds leaving the body would also count as leftovers, and for that reason are potentially defiling.

Let us return to the subject of saliva. Carstairs noted "Our custom of putting our lips to a glass of water, and then setting it back on the table, is distasteful to them, and so is our custom of washing the hands by immersing them in water in a container" (1957:81). He articulates the principle succinctly: ". . . whatever has been in contact with the lips or the inside of the mouth is defiling" (1957:81). This is why "During dinner they are most careful not to drink from one another's water-vessels" (Stevenson 1920:246). Here is another account:

> No Balahi will drain the glass of water . . . from which another person has taken a sip. He will pour the rest away and fill the glass anew. If several persons have to drink from one glass, they usually do not put the mouth to the brim of the glass, but pour the fluid into the mouth holding the glass, at some distance, or they first pour it from the glass into the hollow of the hand and then drink from the hand, But Balahis do not mind drinking water from a river or pond which is also used for bathing or washing clothes" (Fuchs 1950:363).

The reader may see that this drinking procedure is exactly parallel to the untouchable's problems in obtaining water from community wells, described earlier (cf. supra p.13-15).

Saliva appears to be intimately related to one of the most fascinating aspects of leftovers in India, namely, the rules pertaining to food. Dogs and crows are considered polluted in part because they eat human food leftovers (Darling 1934:276). This may explain, in part, why both dogs and crows as food items themselves are extremely low ranking, even below beef (Moffat 1979:114-115). Human scavengers also eat leftovers. One such caste in Madhya Pradesh "visits the houses every morning in order to clean the bathrooms" after which "he gets eatables which are left over from the previous day" (Thaliath 1961:794). The Wisers reported the same thing. Untouchables assemble at a feast "not to share, but to gather up and eat the scraps left on the leaf plates of the party" (Wiser 1971:45-46). The connection with saliva is made explicit by anthropologist Srinivas:

> The Chandala's untouchability was the consequence of his duties on the cremation ground, and of his eating food

rendered impure by its having come into contact with someone else's saliva. (Even today it is regarded as both defiling and degrading to eat such food. To charge someone with having eaten food defiled by another's saliva, is indeed a serious insult). (Srinivas 1984:162; cf. Srinivas 1976:188)

The abhorrence of saliva is of some antiquity. A medieval Tamil tract condemns this belief by having a *Siddha* (saint) address pointed questions to Brahmans. "To those who talk of the impurity of the saliva he puts the question, is it not a fact that the flowers with which you offer *puja* to God, and the honey you taste have been already polluted by the saliva of bees? Has not the milk that you drink already been polluted by the saliva of the calf?" (Hanumanthan 1979:174).

Food leftovers are also an issue with respect to religious practices. One of the most lucid descriptions is the following:

> Now all is ready for the *Offering*. This offering is called *Naivedya* before it has been eaten by the god, but once it has been accepted and eaten by him, it turns into *Prasada*. The Brahmans themselves consider this distinction of great importance, but the writer has never seen the distinction stated anywhere. She may perhaps be able to make it clear to her reader by quoting what her pandit said: "The god eats the offering as *Naivedya*, the worshipper eats it as *Prasada*." (Stevenson 1920:385)
>
> The officiant prepares a tray of food as rich as the temple funds permit, and this he offers to the god as breakfast, but it would be accounted sin if the officiant first breakfasted himself, even though the food for his breakfast had been placed separately on a separate tray. If the officiant had breakfasted himself, the food he offered to the god would not longer be *naivedya* but *ucchista*, a remnant of food ceremonially impure. (Stevenson 1920:391)

The rule is strict. The officiant "must not partake of the particular meal he is going to offer the god until the god has first eaten of it, for if he touched a morsel of it, albeit from a separate dish on a separate tray, the meal offered to the god would be 'a remnant,' not an 'offering,' and so ceremonially impure" (Stevenson 1920:390-391).

Stevenson marked the parallel to human meals: "In the same way in an Indian house a trustworthy cook would not think it respectful to put some food on a separate plate whilst he was cooking and eat from that separate plate before his master had eaten his breakfast" (1920:391).

Here we must distinguish two terms: *jutha* (spelled variously) and *prasad*. "Any food which had touched one's lips became jutha—leavings—and the thought of its being eaten by anyone else was regarded as disgusting" (Carstairs 1957:80). Jutha referred to human food leftovers while prasad refers to food left uneaten by the gods. Carstairs identified prasad "as the jutha of the god" (1957:80) claiming that in southern India the word equivalent to prasad means "the spittle of the god" (1957:80). One essential difference between prasad and jutha is that prasad—food presented to the gods by men but left by the gods to be eaten by humans—can be eaten by anyone irrespective of caste (Davis 1976:21), whereas jutha—human food leftovers—is defiling and can be eaten only by castes ranking lower than the original eaters of the food (Davis 1976:21).

It is hard to convey the disgust with which jutha is regarded. Dubois gave this account:

> To offer a Brahman food on a metal plate which some one had already used, would be considered a deadly insult. Naturally the use of spoons and forks is also forbidden. Fingers are used instead, and Hindus cannot at all understand how we can use these implements a second time, after having put them to our mouths, and allowed them to be touched with saliva. If Hindus should happen to eat dry food or fruits between meals, they break off pieces and throw them into their mouths, fearing if they put them into their mouths with their fingers the latter might be tainted with saliva. (1906:184)

The idea that one's own saliva can be polluting to oneself is also attested by the report from South India that "A Brahman may take snuff, but he should not smoke a cheroot or cigar. When once the cheroot has touched his lips, it is defiled by his saliva, and, therefore, cannot be returned to his mouth. If he could smoke without taking the cheroot out of his mouth all would be well, but unfortunately he cannot. . . ." (Sharrock 1910:9).

Once again we see the same reasoning. Just as toothbrushes cannot be used more than once, just as latrines cannot be used twice without elaborate purification ritual, so metal plates and silverware should not be re-used. Naipaul commented on this as a practice which had survived in the Indian community in Trinidad: "Leaves, to eat your food off, were brahmanically more correct than plates. Leaves were used once and thrown away; plates were used more than once and were technically always polluted, however much you washed them" (1991: 246). It is the body emission, the leftover so to speak, that causes the defilement. Whether it is the possible presence of fecal material on a toilet seat or saliva on a fork or plate, the principle is identical. And it is not just the feces or saliva of others that presents a danger; one's own feces and saliva are a constant threat. Leaf plates (rather than metal plates) can be thrown away after one use; fingers can be thoroughly washed (whereas one never knows how clean an eating utensil like a fork or spoon might be); and food can be more or less thrown into the mouth without the fingers actually touching the inside of the mouth.

There is plenty of ethnographic evidence attesting to the feelings of disgust surrounding the eating of jutha. "There is nothing more degrading in the eyes of Hindu society than the eating of mixed leavings of the food of others" (Briggs 1953:39). "While the Balahis eat the leavings of a dinner of the higher castes, there is no caste so low as to touch the *jhutha* of the Balahis" (Fuchs 1950:368). The repugnance felt toward food leftovers is also expressed in folktales. In a Kannada tale entitled "The Rain King's Wife," a raingod tries to seduce a princess. She refuses, however, to speak to him. "Then he got tired and angry. He said, 'Look here, think carefully. If you do this to me, you'll wander like a beggar, and eat other people's leftovers for food. Think about it.'" (Ramanujan 1997:156). The feelings of repugnance felt toward food leftovers are also manifested in the rules for cleaning both the cooking and serving areas in a household. These areas "should be very carefully cleaned, leaving no specks of left-over foods, whether eaten or not, from the previous cooking, for even one such speck would be sufficient to pollute the entire kitchen and the food cooked in it'" (Khare 1976a:31).

Just as feces is defiling to everyone except the mother of the infant who produces it, so there is one exception to the rule of not eating jutha. The wife is expected to eat her husband's jutha. "After marriage, the wife may, and does, eat off her husband's leaf, after he has finished eating" (Dubois 1906:227, n.1). "As soon as the husband has finished his meal the wife takes hers on the same plate, upon which, as a proof of his affection for her, her husband will leave a few scraps. She, for her part, will show no repugnance at eating the fragments that he has left" (Dubois 1906:247). She shows no aversion just as a mother shows no disgust at cleaning her infant after he has defecated.

There are many other accounts of the wifely duty with respect to jutha. In a book entitled *The Hindoos As They Are* written by Siva-chandra Vasu using the pseudonym Shib Chunder Bose, first published in 1881, we are told: "A married woman considers it no disgrace, but rather an act of merit to eat the remainder of her husband's meal in his absence: so great is the respect in which a husband is held, and so warm the sympathy existing between them. Even an elderly woman, the mother of five or six children, cheerfully partakes of the residue, as if it were the leavings of the gods" (Vasu 1883:76n). Here the partial parallelism between prasad and jutha is implied. The choice of the term *respect* supports anthropologist Harper's decision to call this custom "respect-pollution" saying, ". . . the theme of a wife's subordination toward her husband finds ritual expression in her act of eating from his leaf after he has finished" (1964:181). Marriott also interpreted the wife's eating of her husband's jutha as a marker of socially inferior status: ". . . jutha, that is, food left on plates after eating, is felt to have been polluted by saliva flowing from the mouth of the eater. Such garbage is to be handled in the family only by persons such as wives whose status is thereby marked as inferior to the eater; it may be fed to domestic animals, but among humans outside the family can be given only to Sweepers" (Marriott 1968:142).

Certainly there is a hierarchical aspect to "leftovers." Inferior mortals eat the gods' *prasad*; inferior wives eat their husbands' *jutha*; and disciples eat the leftovers of their guru (Malamoud 1972:14). The paradoxical ambiguity of leftovers is resolved when what is inedible to high status individuals is eaten by persons of lower status, (cf. Malamoud 1972:15; for a ranking of leftover foods, see Khare 1976a:91).

Carstairs offered a bold interpretation of jutha when he suggested it was equivalent to feces (1957:162). Actually, Malamoud, in one of the very few in-depth discussions of leftovers (especially food) in India, cited textual evidence to the effect that a man retained in employment must not be required to handle "leftovers" any more than he would be required to handle a cadaver, urine or excrement (1972:6). But Carstairs may have gone too far when he claimed that when fathers offered their leftover food to their children, these leftovers represented "the faeces of the father." According to Carstairs, "Emotionally, jutha are treated with the same abhorrence as is human excrement" (1957:162). Carstairs' discussion of jutha as paternal feces drew severe criticism from anthropologist Pocock (1961:49-50). The paternal identification may be a bit far-fetched, but in my opinion, it would not be unreasonable to argue that, in the case of the husband's jutha being consumed by the wife, we have a striking analogy to a mother's removing the fecal waste from an infant son.

If one were inclined to take Carstairs' suggestion that jutha is symbolically equivalent to feces at all seriously—which surely most non-Freudians would not—one could conceivably argue that all body emissions, exudates, and exuviae count as leftovers and as such are defiling. Inasmuch as feces is deemed the most defiling if one were to compile a rank-ordering of such body products, then it might not be so unreasonable to construe these various substances, e.g., nasal mucous, as a fecal surrogate or symbolic equivalent.

Leaving aside the question of whether jutha is or is not symbolically equivalent to feces, we may now turn to the issue of the possible connection between the theory of leftovers and the deplorable custom of sati (suttee) or widow burning. Although sati has been declared "dead" (Crawford 1980:84), it has unfortunately not entirely disappeared. On September 4, 1987, an eighteen-year-old widow named Roop Kanwar in Deorala village in Rajesthan "ceremoniously went into flames on the funeral pyre of her deceased husband" in front of "a large crowd, which assembled there to witness this spectacle" and "joined in celebrating the occasion" (Dalal et al 1988:349; Kishwar and Vanita 1987). Admittedly, the number of reported cases of sati is relatively small compared to the figures available from the early nineteenth century. According to Dubois, "In 1817 there were 706 suttees in the Bengal Presidency" (1906:357n). Another statistic is from the same area: "Between 1815, the year when official figures became available on sati, and 1828, the last year before sati was legally prohibited, a total of 7,941 incidents of widow burning had taken place in Bengal alone (not counting those that did not get reported officially)" (Narasimhan 1992:115; cf. Stein 1978:257).

In addition to being clearly inhumane, sati is also sexist (Crawford 1980:84), inasmuch as widows were asked to throw themselves onto their late husbands' funeral pyres, whereas widowers had no such obligation. But the critical question remains: what logic, if any, underlies the custom of sati? It is not enough to say simply that widows cannot remarry (Dubois 1906:210). Why can't they remarry? Widowers can. According to Nandy, since the widow was held to be to blame for her husband's predeceasing her (which was quite unfair in view of the custom of child-marriage, a custom virtually guaranteeing that the husband would predecease his much younger wife), "Sati was . . . an enforced penance, a death penalty through which the widow expiated her responsibility for her husband's death" (1980:9). A widow was held responsible for her husband's death (by sin in a previous life if not in the present" (Stein 1978:255). Incidentally, a sin in a previous life could be construed as a kind of leftover (cf. Malamoud 1972:22; Khare 1976a:101 n.12). Sati was thus "an expression of the culture's deepest fears of and hatred toward—woman and womanhood" (Nandy 1980:8). If this is so, and it is only an opinion, it could well be related to the hostility felt toward the betraying maternal figure of infancy who abruptly ended the long period of infantile indulgence.

Another view is that only faithful wives could commit sati so that failure to do so constituted a self-admission of guilt (Stein 1978:254). ". . . the popular exposition of the law of Karma teaches that, if a wife commits adultery, she will be punished by becoming a widow during seven successive rebirths, and therefore a widow is *ipso facto* an adulteress, detected, exposed and sentenced" (Stevenson 1920:443). Widows thus had a terrible no-win choice: commit sati and die an honorable death or live as a "sinner" whose very presence was defiling or polluting (Stein 1978:255). Interestingly enough, this situation was recognized by Marco Polo near the end of the thirteenth century during his visit to India. After a man died, "his relations proceed, with great triumph and rejoicing, to burn the body; and his wife, from motives of pious regard for her husband, throws herself upon the pile, and is consumed with him. Women who display this resolution are much applauded by the community, as, on the other hand, those who shrink from it are despised and reviled" (Polo 1961:340). There is some thought that the practice was largely restricted to the higher castes (Mazumdar 1978:270; Gandhi 1977:151).

Since a family's honor was involved, a reluctant widow was often encouraged to commit sati. Indeed, the more appropriate term would be homicide rather than mere encouragement. Here is a report from the early part of the twentieth century: "We English believe sati to be extinct; reformers in certain districts of India will tell us differently. They know that there are easy methods of getting rid of an unwanted widow; simply to turn her out of house and home; to push her down a well; to give her poison; to take her on a pilgrimage and either lose her or sell her; or to set fire to her and burn her to death" (Stevenson

1920:207). Since a widow is impure and her presence defiling, burning her to death is the same as is done in some instances to untouchables. It is also the punishment in our tales of crow and sparrow. Something polluted can be purified by fire. Stevenson provided further gruesome detail:

> It is quite simple to soak a heavy wadded quilt in paraffin, to tie a young widow up in it, pour more oil over her, set fire to it and lock her up in a room. Then the neighbors can be told that she either accidentally caught fire when cooking, or like a faithful wife herself committed sati; and only God, "the Judge of the fatherless and the widow," knows on which side the door of that hellish room was locked. Paraffin is cheap—and the family honor has been saved. (Stevenson 1920:208)

This is all very sad, but it does not reveal any connection between sati and jutha. Is there such a connection? Here are a few hints:

> A wife, especially among the socially higher castes, is also required to sacrifice herself for her husband in everyday life, though it is not so drastic as sati. The sacrifice is to serve her husband faithfully. For example, it is a sacrificial action that a wife eats a dinner by using the plate which her husband has used, after serving a meal to him. They think of this action as that of absorbing and removing pollution from her husband so that, if a wife accumulated pollution through this action in her body and ultimately died, this could be equated to sati as the result of everyday efforts of self-sacrifice. (Sekine 1989:37)

A strikingly similar view is articulated by Indian anthropologist Veena Das when she suggested that "the impurity a woman incurs during sexual intercourse is the impurity of a thing partially consumed." She continued, "A woman's body, they say, is made juthi every day" (1985: 4). Das further said "that which has been made jutha by partial use can never attain purity again. Hence . . . the irreversibility of a pollution that a woman is obliged to incur through the process of sexual relations" (1985:4). Das did not refer specifically to widowhood but she mentioned sati: "Just as a woman absorbs in herself the pollution of sexual intercourse, so that the life process may continue, so does a good wife absorb in herself the dangers to her husband. Women blame themselves excessively if a misfortune befalls the husband and may also be blamed by others. The whole notion of sati implies an ascetic life by the wife through which . . . faults, pollution, sin and danger may be internalized by the wife" (1985:4). It is significant that this statement is made by an Indian female anthropologist, clearly an insider.

But perhaps the strongest hint of a connection between sati and jutha comes from a nineteenth-century religious leader from Bombay who opposed the move to legalize widow remarriage. This leader is alleged to have said, "Like a dining leaf used previously by another person, she is unfit to be enjoyed by another person" (Narasimhan 1992:34). Here is the equation of widow and jutha made explicit. "But the real objection of a Brahman to a second marriage is that it offends his idea of chastity. A gift, they say, can only be made once, and as the bride was given to the bridegroom at her wedding, she can never be given a second time to anyone else" (Stevenson 1920:206). Taking all this into account, and keeping in mind the theory of leftovers, we can see that widows are basically culturally defined as "used goods." They are like toothbrushes, eating utensils, and latrines. In this case, it is not saliva that has rendered them "used" as in jutha, but rather male semen. I am in no way defending this cruel sexist view of women as second-class citizens, as objects which can be adjudged defiled and defiling. But once it is understood that widows are like "dining leaves," one can see the logic that ineluctably leads to sati. Fire is a standard conventional means in India of getting rid of a defiling substance or object. One might argue that in some cases when marriages were not physically consummated that the theory of leftovers might not apply, but this is too literal a view. Widows are *de facto* leftovers and, as such, are defiling whether the marriage was physically consummated or not.

## Breaking the Rules

We have seen that leftovers of all kinds are defiling, and that the theory of leftovers can help explain why some castes are considered unclean and some clean. We know, for example, that Dhobi or washermen are low status and ritually impure given that "he is dealing with soiled and ritually impure clothes" (Fuchs 1981:221). But what is on those clothes could, in the present context, be construed as leftovers. Toddy tappers and potters are also low-status castes (Fuchs 1981:238). One is tempted to guess that potters work with clay which is an obvious fecal substitute and it is that activity, or rather substance, that contributes to their low rank. Toddy tappers take liquids from trees, such liquids being considered as analogous to animal body fluids which as previously noted are defiling (cf. Dumont 1980:370 n.41c for an alternative theory). We are told that "professional drummers are polluted as a class because of contact with the skin coverings of their drums" (Emerson 1930:307). Such skin coverings are said to be polluting because they were taken from dead animals and that death as such is polluting. But the skins could also be considered as leftovers just as human hair and sheep's wood could be in the case of barbers and weavers. It should be noted that sheep are not killed when their fleece is sheared. Nor are humans killed when their hair is cut. Thus, the alleged "death" connection would not seem to explain the untouchable status of barbers and weavers.

We have also seen how defiling saliva can be, second only to feces, it would seem. "When speaking to a superior, politeness demands than an inferior should put his right hand before his mouth to prevent any particle of his breath or saliva reaching and defiling him" (Dubois 1906:330). ". . . One should not blow on a fire with one's breath for fear that saliva will pollute it" (Orenstein 1968:124-125). Saliva is even part of the objection to inhaling second-hand smoke. One man explained, "I dislike very much the idea of taking into my lungs smoke which has been in other people's mouths and is saturated with their saliva" (Wood 1962:52).

Yet there are apparently exceptions to the rules governing the ingestion of leftovers. We have already discussed the exceptional case of ingesting the pancha-gavya as a means of purification. In such exceptional cases, the normal rules are broken. What is pure becomes impure; what is impure becomes pure. Consider the following detail reported from Bengal in the 1880s. A bridegroom about to leave his home to collect his bride is instructed by his mother "not to use any other betel than his own." The rationale is explicit: "The object of these instructions is to thwart the intention of his mother-in-law to make him an uxorious husband, a wish in which his mother does not share at all, because it is calculated to diminish his regard for her" (Vasu 1883:56). However, after arriving at the bride's household, "Boys, especially the brother-in-law of the bridegroom, now bring him a couple of betel-nuts, to be cut with a pair of nut-crackers he holds in his hand. He objects and hesitates at first, but no excuse is admitted, no plea heard, he must cut them in the best way he can." (Vasu 1883:56-57). A footnote then adds the following fascinating data: "Even the minutest thing in the domestic economy of a Hindoo family is fraught with meaning: the nuts are kept all-day in the bride's mouth and are saturated with her saliva. When cut by the hand of the bridegroom they are supposed to possess a peculiar virtue. Somehow or other, the bridegroom must be made to use them in spite of the warning of his mother, forbidding him to use them on any account. When used, his love for his wife is supposed to be intensified, which is prejudicial to the interests of his mother" (Vasu 1883:58n). The reporter is surely correct in adjudging the custom "fraught with meaning," but it is doubtful whether he fully understood all the ramifications of that meaning. For one thing, there is a clear-cut Oedipal nuance suggesting that bridegroom must substitute "love" for his new bride in place of his previous "love" for his mother, and moreover this substitution is facilitated by his ingesting a body fluid—in this case the saliva—of his bride. Love is evidently in limited supply such that love for his wife diminishes love for his mother. Later, the bridesmaids play tricks on the new groom. Here is an example:

> They contrive to make him chew the beera or betel which was *first* chewed by the bride, and if he be obstinate enough to refuse in obedience to the warning of his mother, which is often the case, four or five young ladies open his lips and thrust the chewed betel into his mouth. What young man would be so ungallant as to resist them after all that? He must either submit, or bear the opprobrium of a foolish discourteous boy. (Vasu 1883:68)

What we have in this ritual reversal is a play on jutha. In this case, it is the male who must accept the saliva-covered item from the female rather than the other way round. The "test" of the groom with respect to cracking his bride's "nut" (taken from her mouth) with his nutcracker is a symbolic enactment of defloration (cf. Róheim 1954). But our primary concern here is the breaking of the normal rule with respect to the ingestion of someone else's saliva.

Even more striking is a case reported by Dubois. According to him (1906:132), there was a group of pilgrims who sought a certain guru: "I have been informed by some of these pilgrims themselves, that the more enthusiastic amongst them watch for the moment when the old guru is about to expectorate, when they stretch out their hands, struggling as to who shall have the happiness and good luck to catch the superfluous fluid which the holy man ejects." Saliva, in this case, is evidently not defiling at all, but rather a desideratum. Perhaps it is a case of religious devotees seeking to show their devotion to a higher personage, one means of so doing consisting of ingesting a normally defiling substance. In sum, by lowering their status or rank, they are simultaneously increasing the social distance between them and their revered guru. The same cultural logic presumably underlies the practice of "drinking the bath water of the guru" (Weber 1958:384 n.44), and even paying for the privilege of so doing.

Dubois discussed another type of religious fanatic he observed (1906;520): "Some of these fanatics profess to conquer every feeling of disgust that is innate in a human being. They will even go so far as to eat human ordure without evincing any dislike. Instead of treating these degraded practices with the horror and contempt that they merit, the Hindus regard them with respect and honour, true to their custom of admiring everything that astonishes them." Possibly the ingestion of feces, which surely constitutes a breaking of the normal rules governing the ingestion of leftovers, is like the above example of swallowing the guru's saliva, that is, it is a sanctioned technique in self-effacement.

One of the most blatant violations of the rules against touching saliva among other taboos is described by Dubois (1906:286-287) in his account of one of the "disgusting religious orgies" he so meticulously depicts. In these orgies, not only do men and women eat meat and drink alcoholic beverages, but they transgress the normal saliva prohibition. I cannot possibly improve upon Dubois' vivid word picture: "In this orgy called *sakti-puja*, the *pujari*, or sacrificer who is generally a Brahman, first of all tastes the various kinds of meats and liquors himself, then gives the others permission to devour the rest. Men and women thereupon begin to eat greedily, the same piece of meat passing from mouth to mouth, each person taking a bite until it is finished. Then they start afresh on another joint, which they gnaw in the same manner, tearing the meat out of each other's mouths. When all the meat has been consumed, intoxicating liquors are passed round, every one drinking without repugnance out of the same cup." In this apparent ritual reversal, the rules of normal behavior are obviously in abeyance. But this elaborate parody or caricature does serve to underscore the existence of these rules. It is perhaps an example of the proverb "The exception proves the rule."

The most defiling "leftover" is, of course, feces. We have seen that the caste of sweepers who deal with the removal of human feces is the lowest-ranking caste, and that animals that eat human feces, animals such as domestic chickens and pigs are scorned for that very reason. In that context, we can understand why accusing someone of eating human feces would be an especially grave insult. The reader may recall that in one version of our second tale, crow was referred to insultingly as "excrement-mouth" (see supra p.44). Interestingly enough, we find comparable epithets in Indian children's folklore. A girl who insists upon playing with boys who do not want her to do so may chase her away with the line: "A girl among boys is a shit-eater" (Vatuk 1970:274). Among children in western Uttar Pradesh in the 1960s, one of the most popular curse words was "excrement eater" (Vatuk 1970:276).

Since Indian folklorists with few exceptions tend to be as prudish as folklorists in other parts of the world, it is not easy to find documentation of "obscene" children's folklore in India. One can only adduce occasional anecdotal data in such instances. Beals described a mother's interaction with her child which includes a pseudo-curse, "May you eat dirt" (1962:20), and we do know that in India "dirt" usually refers to feces rather than to dust or grime or earth (Chakraborty and Banerji 1974:277). Freeman reported an adult example (1979:52): "A Bauri insultingly tells a Brahman who cheats him that if he is so greedy for the Bauri's property, why doesn't he also eat the Bauri's excrement?"

There is some evidence that the insult is not entirely metaphorical. When anthropologist Kathleen Gough claimed that in some Tanjore criminal cases, the offender was asked to drink cow dung as a punishment and occasionally in severe cases "to drink human dung," she was promptly criticized by T. N. Madan who accused her of drawing a hasty conclusion. He recommended that "Foreign investigators should check their data and verify their conclusions before they run to the printing press" (1955:132). Stung by this accusation, Gough was quick to reply, quoting her informants on this matter. She ended her effective rebuttal by suggesting that "Madan would have done well to check my report carefully with a number of Tanjore villagers before he hastened to accuse a foreign investigator of negligence in the reporting of data" (1957:234).

Eating excrement would certainly be an extreme example of breaking the rules of the pollution complex. It would violate the principle of the absolute separation of mouth and anus which is also at the heart of the left and right hand rules. It is analogous to beating someone on the head with a shoe. Time and again, we are told that human excreta are the most defiling of any body emission (Singh 1966:131). Carstairs probably said it in the most succinct fashion: "Any secretion from inside of the body is defiling, but the most defiling of all is human excrement" (1957:81). And it was also Carstairs to his eternal credit who was the first after Berkeley-Hill's 1921 essay to see the possible connection between feces and caste. "Beneath the concern about defilement lay a preoccupation with the noxious properties of human faeces, the arch-contaminant, which was associated with personal and social degradation" (1957:107). To be sure, Carstairs did not spell out in great detail the connection between feces and untouchability, but he certainly understood the critical importance of traditional toilet training: "That Hindus are unobsessional and yet pre-occupied with this topic of faecal contamination is attributable to the fact that in infancy their training in cleanliness is gentle, leisurely and unemphasized" (1957:164). Carstairs did not sufficiently take into account the earliness of the initiation of toilet training (three months) nor did he realize the crucial factor of the crackdown phase at the age of five years. Because of this, Carstairs may have overestimated the effect of what he and others have considered to be lenient toilet training. It is, of course, lenient toilet training, but as discussed earlier, it is tempered by the earliness of the training and the later crackdown. In this regard, I am not certain that Carstairs was altogether correct when he claimed that "Hindus are unobsessional." It is always dangerous to assign any psychological attribute to an entire people—this was Ruth Benedict's mistake in her classic *Patterns of Culture,* when she used psychiatric terms such as "paranoia" and "megalomania" to refer to the Kwakiutl Indians (1946:169, 195). Still, the heavy burden of rules governing Hindu behavior might appropriately be construed as a possible example of "obsessional" character.

One of the relatively few discussions of phobic behavior in India seems to me to be pretty obviously derived from toilet training techniques. There is a curious ritual termed *suchi-bai* in Bengali—the term is translated as "purity-mania" (Chakraborty and Banerji 1975:213). In Marathi also, individuals are said to "suffer" from "ritual purity," such individuals often providing occasions for humor (Apte 1988). Examination of no less than sixty cases of *suchi-bai* yielded the following array of symptoms: "washing too often, not eating anywhere outside, changing of street clothes (own and sometimes compulsorily for all family members); washing of money (including currency notes); bathing for four hours twice a day; hanging out street clothes outside on a tree and entering house naked; hopping while walking (to avoid touching anything dirty in the streets); remaining immersed in the holy river for the best part of the day; sprinkling of cowdung water on all visitors" (Chakraborty and Banerji 1975:214). To be fair, this list refers, of course, to extreme behavior, as was indicated in the several case histories of *such-bai* reported, e.g., "An unmarried girl of twenty was brought to the clinic as she had stopped eating to avoid defecation. . . . She said, "I always had a sense of disgust regarding feces, that's why I kept myself clean and observed all the rules. . . . I would wash for hours without a thought in mind, it is only recently I am trying to stop myself but I can't" (Chakraborty and Banerji 1975:215). Noteworthy is the patient's apparent recognition of the "rules" that she was at great pains to observe.

On the other hand, it is sometimes difficult in any culture to draw a firm line between "obsessive" or extreme behavior and ordinary everyday "normal" behavior. For instance, in 1971 in rural Gujurat, an old woman "was observed washing the coins that she received from an untouchable. It was also the custom that currency notes from the untouchables were touched [only] after they were purified by sprinkling water over them" (Desai 1976:125). Is washing money including currency notes an example of obsessive behavior or it in fact "custom"? Either way, it seems to me to relate directly to toilet training. The money-feces equation is found cross-culturally (cf. Dundes 1984:81-83), and thus from a psychoanalytic perspective, it makes perfect sense to feel the necessity of washing "filthy lucre" to make it clean.

The proverb "Poverty resides in the anus of the Brahman" could refer to the Brahman's need to rid himself of all feces (wealth) (Parry 1985:621), but in any event, it certainly links the themes of wealth and feces or rather poverty and the lack of feces.

Perhaps the most salient evidence for an Indic cloacal cacoethes comes from the formal practice of yoga. A number of the prescribed breathing exercises and postures tend to focus on the anus. This was pointed out by Berkeley-Hill in his 1921 essay when he observed: "we have an exquisite manifestation of the process of 'sublimation,' in this case the conversion of the impulse to control the sphincter ani, especially in its relation to the passage of flatus into a most elaborate quasi-philosophical system" (1921:311). Writer Arthur Koestler in his discussion of "Yoga Unexpurgated" feigned reluctance to speak about "the painful subject of the Hindu obsession with the bowel functions which permeates religious observances and social customs" (1961:87). Referring to the *Hatha Yoga Pradipika* and especially the *Gheranda Samhita*, Koestler reminds us of some of the recommended techniques to be utilized in cleansing various parts of the digestive tract. For example, the stomach may be cleaned "by swallowing a cloth about four inches wide and twenty-two and a half feet long, and then pulling it out" (1961:87;) cf. Digambarji and Gharote 1978:18). Another technique termed "Varisara-Dhouti" consists of the following instruction: "Fill the mouth with water down to the throat, and then drink it slowly; and then move it through the stomach forcing it downwards expelling it through the rectum" (Koestler 1961:88; Digambarji and Gharote 1978:8). The adept is further told, "This process should be kept very secret. It purifies the body." One other example should suffice: "Standing in navel-deep water, one should push out the Sakti-nadi (rectum) and wash it with hands till the filth is being removed. . . . Having washed the Nadi clean, one should draw it in again (into the abdomen). This (method of) cleaning should be kept a secret. It is not easily available even to the Gods" (Digambarji and Gharote 1978:11). Koestler translated Sakti-nadi as "long intestines" rather than "rectum" (1961:88). Koestler also spoke of "reverse procedures" known as basti or "Yoga enemas." Jala-basti, he noted, "consists in squatting in a tub of water navel-high and sucking the water up through the rectum" (1961:88). This would appear to be a prima facie case of attempting to move internal "pollution" outside the body. The stipulation of maintaining secrecy suggests that even the practitioners recognize that these recommended postures and exercises are aberrant behavior bordering on the bizarre.

One last comment on the "obsession" question is provided by the following anecdotal evidence:

> Notwithstanding current British fashions in breakfast foods, digestion, indigestion (*ajiran*) and constipation (*kabza*) strike the outsider as something of an *obsession* [my emphasis] of Benarasi Brahman culture. I recall occasions on which I have been to visit some learned Pandit to discuss the ultimate bliss of union with the absolute only to find myself spending the afternoon listening to a meticulous account of the state of his bowels. (Parry 1985:626)

The implicit moral would appear to be that in India eschatology can easily lead to scatology!

## Gypsy Defilement as Marginal Survival

Assuming that by now the reader—if he or she has managed to get this far in this essay—is persuaded that the so-called pollution-complex in India, especially as it relates to caste and untouchability, is connected to a fear of feces contamination, a fear resulting from the paradoxical mixture of lenient toilet training with early initiation of such, plus an abrupt and traumatic "crackdown" occurring when a child is approximately five years old, that same reader might wonder just how old this elaborate folk belief complex is. How far back in time does it go, and is there any way of determining its antiquity?

In order to attempt an approximate answer to this question, I shall utilize an interesting folkloristic concept called "marginal survival." The concept seems to have been coined by anthropologist Ralph Linton as part of his general theory of diffusion. In his textbook *The Study of Man*, first published in 1936, Linton set forth two principles of diffusion. The first was that "other things being equal, elements of culture will be taken up first by societies which are close to their points of origin and later by societies which are more remote or which have less direct contacts" (1936:328-329). The second principle is that of "marginal survivals" according to which the "original" form of a culture trait may have died out or been replaced at its point of origin but survives more or less intact on the periphery or margins of the diffusional area (1936:329). To illuminate the principle, Linton turned to the image of "ripples sent out by dropping a stone into still water. The last ripples will still be moving outward when the center has once more become quiet" (1936:330). Marginal survival is really part of what used to be termed "Age-and-Area Theory" in anthropology (cf. Hultkrantz 1960: 24-25). One of the postulates of this general theory, which argued essentially that the more widely diffused a culture trait is, the older it may be assumed to be, assumed that "the traits lying at any given moment on the marginal or peripheral belt of a geographical distribution are to be interpreted by the historian of primitive, historyless cultures, as relatively old, while those lying close to or at the center are to be regarded as relatively new" (Hodgen 1942:347).

Folklorists—with their longstanding commitment to the comparative method—have found the principle of marginal survival of some value. One reason for this is that immigrant groups often retain in their folklore particular items that have long since disappeared from the original homeland of these immigrants. Representative discussions in the folklore scholarship include Bruno Nettl's 1957 essay "The Hymns of the Amish: An Example of Marginal Survival" and Warren E. Roberts' 1960 paper "A Spaniolic-Jewish Version of Frau Holle," which suggests a Spanish-Jewish text of Aarne-Thompson tale type 480, "The Spinning-Women by the Spring." "The Kind and the Unkind Girls", collected in the Balkans or Palestine and published in 1947, contains archaic traits from pre-1500 Spain, the time when the Jews were expelled from that country.

In the present instance, we are not claiming that the pollution complex in India has died out by any means, but we wondered to what extent, if any, traces of this complex might be found among contemporary Gypsies. There seems little doubt that the origin of the Gypsies was India, but their exact location in India and the precise date of their departure from their homeland are uncertain. Censensus suggests an approximate date of 1000 A.D. for the departure and the beginning of a near-worldwide diaspora. I should mention that the Gypsiology scholarship is as massive as that devoted to caste and it is even more daunting due to the fact that inasmuch as Gypsies have settled is so many countries, the scholarship is written in a bewildering variety of languages. At least most of the caste scholarship is readily available in English. In any event, I do not intend to give anything like a full ethnographic description of modern Gypsy cultures. Instead, I shall cite what I consider to be a few relevant features of that culture or rather cultures—Gypsy culture varies from country to country. At this point, there is no one single Gypsy culture.

Generally speaking, wherever Indians have migrated, they have tended to take some form of caste with them (cf. Schwartz 1967; Ramasamy 1984). However, the documentation of caste among Indians living outside of India, that is, among overseas Indians, has not to my knowledge been systematically carried out with respect to Gypsies. The present inquiry is not so much concerned with caste per se, as with Gypsy notions of defilement and Gypsy attitudes toward the body and body products.

According to Carol Miller, "The ideology of defilement, or marime . . . is pervasive to Rom categories of belief and thought, and extends to all areas of Rom life in some way. . . ." (1975:41; for valuable surveys of the Gypsy concept of pollution, see Sutherland 1975:255-287; and Okeley 1983a:77-104). Notes Miller, "Body orifices that give access to the inner body are defensively guarded, some from further pollution and some from any pollution at all. Because the process of ingestion breaches the margins of the inviolate body area, eating is a delicate and closely regulated matter" (1975:42). Other observers confirm this. "Anything taken into the body for its sustenance must be ritually clean. . . . The outer body must be kept separate from the inner: even a person's shadow can pollute food" (Okeley 1975:60; cf. Weyrauch and Bell 1993:350). The detail among English Gypsies that "Food can even be polluted by a shadow, especially that of a non-Gypsy" (Okeley 1983b:252) certainly is reminiscent of Indic fears of pollution caused by the shadow of an untouchable. The shadow's ill effect is, of course, a further example of negative contagious magic, the shadow being connected to, or considered part of, a polluting individual. If the shadow falls on food, it is in terms of contagious magic the same as if the person whose shadow it is had touched the polluted individual or the latter's food.

Again from English Gypsies, ". . . the mouth is a possibly dangerous point of entry into the inner body, and must absorb only ritually clean food" (Okeley 1975:68, 76, 78; cf. 1983b:253). In the fundamental distinction between the inside of the body and the outside, "The outer skin with its discarded scales, accumulated dirt, by-products such as hair, and waste such as faeces, are all potentially polluting" (Okeley 1975:60; 1983b:253). Among Finnish Gypsies, the desire to keep mouth separate from anus, food separate from feces, is manifested by the revulsion of having a kitchen situated next to a bathroom in modern low-cost housing. In such a case, "Water for cooking cannot be taken from a toilet faucet even if it might be the only tap for the entire household. In that case water must be fetched from some other place, for instance a near-by cafe" (Viljanen-Saira 1980:225).

We thus find in Gypsy cultures the same concern as in India with keeping the mouth and the anus totally separate. We see this, also for example, in the Gypsy attitude toward cats and dogs. "Unclean animals must never be allowed to enter the trailer. This category includes cats and most dogs. . . . Cats and dogs are unclean because they break the rules of cleanliness; they lick their fur, taking their outer bodily dirt into their mouths and inner body. A cat is especially dirty because, as a Gypsy explained to me, "It licks its paws after burying its dirt" (Okeley 1983b:252, 253). This attitude confirms an earlier report from a study of the concept of uncleanness among English Gypsies: "We should say as it was *moxadi* to eat after a dog, and so it is, cause dogs has got dirty ways to 'em" (Thompson 1922:20, n.3). A footnote explains that it is the fact that dogs and cats lick themselves all over which is the chief reason why Gypsies regard these animals are *moxadi* (cf. Acton 1971: 112). *Moxadi* or *mochadi* is an alternate term for "polluted" or "defiled," which, according to one source, is cognate with "an Indian-derived word makhardo, meaning smeared" (Weyrauch and Bell 1993:342, n.63). If this etymology is at all accurate, the connotations of "smeared" might well be related to an anal origin of the pollution concept (cf. Acton 1971:134 n.9).

The inside-outside dichotomy is manifested with respect to other animals. For example, among British Gypsies, we are informed that "snakes were particularly disgusting and dangerously contaminating because of the way they shed their skins, thus converting the inside into the outside, and because they ate other animals whole devouring their dirty skins" (Fonseca 1995:106). A truly remarkable human instance of the inside-outside distinction is the English Gypsy account of a man who, despite going to a "clean" baker, insisted upon stripping off the outer crust and eating only the interior of a baked item (Okeley 1983a:84).

The inside-outside dichotomy is found not only in the Gypsy view of the body, but in their conception of space as well. In the spatial arena, the inside must be kept clean and pure, separate from the dirty outside. "Toilet functions must be done a distance from the trailer. The interior of a trailer is a central focus of purity" (Okeley 1983b:252). So accordingly defecation must take place outside, not inside. Apparently, "Germans often complain that Gypsy refugees urinate and defecate outdoors" (Weyrauch and Bell 1993:346 n.90). Gypsies find objectionable the non-Gypsy custom of having chemical toilets inside trailers (Okeley 1983b:251).

The subject of toilets leads logically to the topic of toilet training, which we believe to be so critical with respect to the formation and perpetuation of the Indic pollution complex. Unfortunately, despite the enormous literature devoted to the Gypsies (e.g., Tong 1995), there is scant ethnographic detail concerning Gypsy toilet training practices. What little data exists would tend to support the marginal survival argument proposed. Anthropologist Rena C. Gropper, in her study of New York City Gypsies remarked, "Gypsies do not rush toilet training, and they attach no shame to a child's body parts or excretions" (1975:55). In another statement, "Gradualness is also the keynote of toilet-training. . . . Babies are exempted from rules of marime, and their physiological requirements are not considered polluting. It is taken for granted that babies will soil whoever holds them, and no one fusses when it happens. . . . Toilet training, however, once children have learned it, is expected to be honored in full" (Gropper 1975:133). Certainly these tantalizingly brief comments seem to conform to Indic practice.

As the interior of the body and trailer must be kept clean, so the Gypsy campground is subject to the same rules. ". . . The center of the camp may be treated as an area of cleanliness comparable to the interior of the trailer. Otherwise the ground outside is seen as no-man's land and a working area, over which the Gypsies have no control. There will be little attempt to claim it through orderliness and cleanliness" (Okeley 1983b:253). This surely seems analogous to the situation in India. The marked contrast between dirty outside and clean inside has been noted by a number of observers. Ambroise, in an interesting analysis of Hindu space, refers to a distinction between "within" and "without," which allegedly applies to both village and house. Moreover, "The notion of 'within' and 'without' in the spatial notion of the house structures the state of cleanliness. The space within the house is kept clean but just outside the house they do not bother to keep it clean. . . ." (Ambroise 1982:340). Similarly, Bassa remarked that even in makeshift dwellings without plumbing, it was "immaculately clean inside, especially in the kitchen" (1978:340). Roland too commented that while apartments or flats were well taken care of, hallways and other public spaces were not (1980:80). In applying the distinction to the individual body-ego, Roland suggested that "outside the family, it is a no-man's land" (1980:80), a turn of phrase used above to refer to the Gypsy spatial exterior.

In addition to having a strong categorical distinction between inside and outside, Gypsies also distinguish the upper part of the body from the lower part. According to "Gypsy law, the human body is both pure and impure. The waist is the equator, or dividing line. The lower body is *marime* because the genital areas and the feet and legs may cause pollution and defilement. The upper body is fundamentally pure and clean. Any unguarded contact between the lower and upper bodies is *marime*" (Weyrauch and Bell 1993:343). The standard study of defilement among American Gypsies makes a similar point (Miller 1975:42): "Any contact between the lower half of the body, particularly the genitals which are conceptually the ultimate source of *marime*, and the upper body is forbidden" One cannot help but think of a passage in the

*Laws of Manu* dating perhaps from some two thousand years ago: "The orifices of the body above the navel are all pure, but those below are impure, as are the defilements that slip out of the body" (Doniger and Smith 1991:113 [5:132].)

Many remarkable parallels in Gypsy cultures to the Indian pollution complex exist, but I shall confine myself to citing just a few more representative ones. An Alsatian Gypsy "never speaks to anyone in the morning before he has washed his mouth . . . to do this, he must undergo an act of purification, and this he does by thoroughly rinsing his mouth as soon as he gets out of bed . . . and uses running or fresh water . . . to do so" (Rao 1975:153). This is strongly reminiscent of elaborate Hindu mouth-rinsing rituals. Moreover, Alsatian Gypsies think that non-Gypsies "are very dirty as they try and wash themselves in their own filth, when they use bathtubs, etc.," and they don't use swimming pools either (Rao 1975:153). Among Finnish Gypsies, after a Gypsy takes a bath, he or she has to wash his or her hands "before touching anything, because by washing and dressing oneself one had touched both his/her ritually unclean parts of his/her body and his/her ritually unclean clothes (underwear, footwear, etc.)" (Viljanen-Saira 1980:225). Even more startling, a Scottish "traveller" woman remembers being humiliated as a girl by being beaten with a shoe (Whyte 1979:52).

Here are several other possible marginal survivals: "Since gypsies collect rags and scraps [that is, waste products!] picking through materials thrown away by the majority society, they are considered scavengers" (Okeley 1975:60). Gypsies in Philadelphia allegedly have castes classified according to occupation, and "They eat with the fingers" (Bonos 1942:262,268). Gypsies prefer to eat with their hands rather than use forks or other utensils which might have been used by non-Gypsies (Sutherland 1977:380; Silverman 1991:113). In English Gypsy tradition, "Any left-overs from meals are instantly jettisoned. . . . Nothing once cooked or prepared is saved" (Okeley 1983a:84). Among Spanish Gypsies, "A widower may marry again after some years, but ideally a widow should not marry again" (San Román 1975:185). Among Alsatian Gypsies, ". . . such things as fire are intrinsically pure and can never become impure" (Rao 1975:149-150). Among English Gypsies, we are told, "Fire is considered to be the suitable purifier for *mochadi* articles . . . ." (Okeley 1975:65). Now we are right back to the end of the Crow and Sparrow tales with the application of fire to the buttocks of the untouchable Crow!

Occasionally we find Gypsy customs that have obviously continued a longstanding tradition, but whose rationale has been eroded by time and failing memory. For example, among English Gypsies, Thompson reported that they wouldn't "touch a knife that had been used for skinning a horse. Like the German Gypsies, they regarded it as unclean. Precisely why they did so I could not discover; nor anything more, except that they counted the horse a clean animal, but looked with suspicion on all butchers' knives" (1929:38). The same taboo is found among Polish Gypsies (Ficowski 1951:127). In India, touching the skin of a dead animal is considered polluting, the skin being a sort of outside leftover in terms of this essay.

But even if a Gypsy custom is not well understood by contemporary Gypsies, its very existence is of interest. The reader should keep in mind that Gypsies have had little or no contact with their "original" Indian homeland for a thousand years! The fact that portions of the pollution complex could survive intact that long despite centuries of wandering and persecution is a testament to the strength of Gypsy folklore. While Gypsies tend to regard non-Gypsies as potentially polluting, that is, as a kind of untouchable, there is one object that supposedly Gypsies will not touch themselves. Perhaps the reader can already guess what that object might be. Here is a fascinating quotation from a Gypsy autobiography: "Plumbing is a trade forbidden to Gypsies by their own law. A Gypsy man would be defiled by handling toilet fixtures and would run the grave risk of being socially ostracized. Gypsies don't even sit on a toilet seat but sort of squat over it" (Lee 1972:21). Here we have a Canadian Gypsy articulating in no uncertain terms the fear of contamination by contact with feces and even the reluctance to use latrines which we remarked on earlier in this essay. What an extraordinary example of a marginal survival after a thousand years or more! Also relevant is the reference to social ostracism. The Gypsy concept of *marime* means both defilement and social disgrace. The disgrace may be so great as to lead a to expulsion from the group. "The Rom *marime* is outcasted from social and political affairs" (Miller 1975:51). We know that expulsion from a caste is also found in India—as indicated by the word "outcaste" itself. Impurity from contact with an unclean caste person can be grounds for expulsion or being beaten with a shoe can also lead to excommunication which "may extend for twelve years" (Briggs 1953:169,173). Incidentally, this last source is from a study of the Doms who some think may well be the ancestors of the

Roms (Briggs 1953:265). In any case, according to our Canadian Gypsy, non-Gypsies are hired if a plumbing job is necessary "since a toilet, to us, is *marimé* (defiled) and any Gypsy man who touches one automatically becomes *pokelimé* or polluted" (Lee 1967:43; cf. Weyrauch and Bell 1993:346, 350, n.114).

What happens to someone who is socially ostracized? In England, "A law-breaker is allowed to travel with the band, but no one must drink from the same glass as he, nor eat from the same plate, nor use the same knife, fork, or spoon" (Thompson 1922:40, n.2). Law-breaker in this sense refers to someone the group has declared moxadi or defiled. Again, this all sounds so very familiar.

There are yet more parallels between the Indic and Gypsy cultures. For example, we are told among American Gypsies that "Blowing is also a curative and cleansing act. Blowing on cuts helps them to heal. . . ." (Sutherland 1975:265). This is surely reminiscent of Indic practice (see supra p.107). Albanian Gypsies were shocked and amused to see a Western woman visitor use a toothbrush (Fonseca 1995: 62), a reaction not unlike the Hindu abhorrence of the same item (see supra p.71). There is even a hint that English Gypsies indulged in a custom called "lustering," which involved widows being burned with their dead husbands, a clear echo of sati (Fonseca 1995:106).

It would be ridiculous and absurd to think that all of the above Gypsy parallels to the Indian pollution complex were just a matter of coincidence. This is no instance of polygenesis or independent invention. We do know, after all, through linguistic and other evidence that the Gypsies' ancestors did in fact come from India. What the Gypsy concept of defilement as a marginal survival means is that the folk belief complex I have sought to describe in this essay is not of recent invention. Moreover, the suggestion that it has survived more or less intact for a thousand years or so is an incredible testament to its obvious central importance in the lives of those peoples who are under its sway. Given its demonstrated tenacity, one might wonder just difficult it may prove to alter it, assuming one might wish to do so in the name of social reform.

## Conclusions

As we approach the end of this essay, it might be useful to review what we have learned. We began with a consideration of caste with its confusing jumble of Varna and Jati systems. The fixed four categories of Varna plus the lowly untouchables resulting in only five distinct caste subsets is one of two overlapping paradigms, with another hierarchically arranged set of hundreds of Jatis or subcastes being the second. While local or regional groupings of castes may vary, the overall picture of Brahmans at the top and untouchables at the bottom seemed fairly constant throughout India.

Next followed a brief overview of untouchability with examples of the devastating restrictions it entails, e.g., on drawing water from wells, entering temples and other public areas, on avoiding contact with higher ranked castes, etc.

We then presented two folktales involving a crow and a sparrow. The idea was to see if these tales could provide any access to the folk belief complex underlying caste and untouchability. The first tale, Aarne-Thompson tale type 2030B, Crow Must Wash His Bill In Order To Eat With Other Birds, a tale found really only in India, turned out to demonstrate a unique oicotypical feature. Whereas most cumulative formula tales with interdependent linking members include a final section in which all the links become undone or unravelled, that is, where the protagonist succeeds in attaining his or her goal, there is no such section in AT 2030B. Instead the poor crow never does get to eat a communal meal with sparrow. Despite going to a lot of trouble, crow is never able to wash itself clean. Indeed, the very ending of the tale is somewhat peculiar inasmuch as the crow dies, typically by fire. The punishment seems somewhat severe as it is not totally clear that the crow did anything wrong to merit such punishment. In retrospect, one can see that the tale is a truly accurate folk model of the caste-untouchability system. Crow's untouchability is immutable; the pollution of a crow is inherent—it is ascribed, not achieved. It cannot be altered. A crow can never be clean enough to share a meal with a sparrow any more than an untouchable can ever be clean enough to share a meal with a Brahman. One of the prescribed ways for treating defilement consists of undergoing an ordeal by fire. So the end of the tale makes perfect cultural sense after all.

The second tale of crow and sparrow, a cognate of Aarne-Thompson tale type 123, The Wolf and the Kids (which is the same as Aarne-Thompson tale type 333, The Glutton [Red Riding Hood], except that it has all animal dramatis personae, and the villain comes to the victim's house instead of the other way round), gives us another important clue as to the underlying basis of caste and untouchability. In this tale, crow does eventually gain access to sparrow's abode, which, leads to a transformation of food into feces inside the house. Sparrow or more precisely her children are duped into touching crow's feces after which crow is punished by fire once again. Crow's "crime" consists of filling a *food* container with *feces*, thereby violating the rule of separation of mouth and anus. The ensuing discussion of both tales reveals why crow is an appropriate foil figure, associated as crow is with feces and pollution.

Since the standard literary charter for the Varna system contains a body origin of caste myth that inexplicably fails to account for untouchables, it is suggested that the myth originally did account for untouchables from a body part, namely, the anus. This hypothesis is supported by the demonstration of the pervasiveness of the ritual number five in Indian culture as well as to a curious literary reference to a caste being "born from the rear-end." The body metaphor also includes a number of cross-cutting binary oppositions: head versus foot (top versus bottom); right (hand) versus left (hand); front (mouth) versus back (anus); and inside versus outside. The clean set includes head, right, front and inside; the polluted set includes foot, left, back, and outside. The body metaphorical paradigm confirms the association of untouchables with feces.

A survey of defecation habits amplified the paradigm with special reference to the "inside" versus "outside" distinction. The outside world (where one defecates) must be kept absolutely separate and distinct from the inside world (where one lives). The toilet facilities must stay outside well away from the eating/kitchen facilities inside.

After a brief discussion of the state of Freudian theory in India where one finds the same kind of popular and academic distrust of psychoanalysis as is common elsewhere, we considered previous anthropological attempts to explain the rationale underlying the pollution complex. The mere statement that there is a pure-impure opposition connected to caste is at best descriptive; it is hardly analytic.

Before examining traditional toilet training in India, we cited both Gandhi and Tagore to suggest that the equation of sweeper/scavenger and mother was proposed independent of Freud. Those few psychoanalysts or anthropologists who did consider Freudian "anal character" in connection with India did not really discuss caste or untouchability per se. They typically erred by assuming that the exact same "complex" would be or should be found in India that was reported in the West. When it was not, they wrongly concluded that Freudian theory simply did not apply to India.

Toilet training in India turns out to be quite different from toilet training in the West. Although there was consensus that Indian toilet training was more lenient than in the West, this is a half-truth. Yes, it is more lenient, especially since it can take up to five years to complete. But the issue is more complex, inasmuch as toilet training is begun much earlier than in the West, e.g., at age three months, and it ends much more abruptly with a "crackdown" at age five when the full panoply of rules governing the pollution complex falls upon a previously indulged infant/child. It was suggested that it was this mixed message of Indian toilet training that is closely related to the pollution complex. On the one hand, adults are free to defecate outside wherever they wish—just as infants are free to do the same, but on the other hand, they are required eventually to cleanse themselves (as opposed to having mother or mother surrogate do it) in a prescribed ritual fashion, before returning inside. Later in life, if adults go "outside" the country, e.g., to Europe or America, to be educated, they must be purified by ingesting the five products of the cow before being fully accepted "inside" the country once again. It is surely no coincidence that the two primary areas of indulgence in Indian infancy: the breast providing food and the relaxed attention to elimination are both reflected in adult life with respect to oral and anal taboos.

As the mother is the principal agent of infant care in the Indian context, an attempt is made using this fact to explain some of the mystery surrounding the treatment of cows in India. As the mother is not defiled by the infant's body products, so in later life, the adult is not defiled by the mother (cow)'s body products. Quite the contrary, cow dung is not defiling at all but is considered to be an efficacious cleansing agent, even by well-educated Indians. Moreover, it was suggested that the denial of oral aggression toward the maternal breast might possibly account for the taboo against eating beef as an adult.

The attitude toward feces is then set in a larger context of a theory of leftovers. According to this notion, anything produced by the body or separated from the body can—through the principle of negative contagious magic—be defiling. So it is that saliva, for example, is almost as polluting as feces. Whether it is a ranking of castes based upon who accepts food from whom, or who accepts the food leavings from whom, or whether it is the exceptional case of a wife's being required to eat the jutha from her husband's plate, the theory of defiling leftovers seems fairly consistent. The theory also helps explain why certain castes whose occupations involve handling "leftovers" such as skins, hair, or wood, are considered untouchable. The theory is then applied to the awful custom of sati, arguing that widows are defiling because they too are defined as leftovers. Once touched by male semen, they cannot be "re-used" by some other male. Moreover, the custom of burning impure widows conforms to the standard way of removing defilement by fire, as was the case in both tales of the Crow and the Sparrow.

Then, after a brief demonstration of how the "rules" governing such leftovers as saliva and feces can be illustrated by exceptional cases when the rules are ritually broken, we attempt to show the longevity of the folk belief complex in question as well as its remarkable tenacity by a cursory sampling of Gypsy ethnography. Most of the salient features of the Indian pollution complex would appear to have been preserved as marginal survivals in Gypsy cultures, even in the United States and Canada. This would make the pollution complex at least one thousand years old, and it is more than likely that it is nearly twice that old. But establishing the age of the complex is not the goal of this essay.

The goal was to illuminate the nature of caste and untouchability in India by trying to ascertain the folk belief complex that underlies this unusual form of human social organization. I wish to make clear that I am not claiming that the particulars of Indian infant/child toilet training "cause" the caste/untouchability system. It is always a mistake to assume that any one element of culture is logically prior to all others. From an ontogenetic perspective, it may be reasonable to say that an infant's conditioning in his or her experience of toilet training prepares that individual for the adult preoccupation with the pollution complex, but ultimate origin questions invariably become chicken and egg. If we assume that the crackdown at age five is one of the precipitating factors in the development of individual children in India, the issue would then turn on what is the origin of the crackdown? In other words, it is an oversimplification to say that infantile conditioning "causes" adult personality. The reason for this is that infantile conditioning does not occur in a cultural vacuum. Where does any tradition of infantile conditioning come from? It is, after all, imposed by parents, by adults. But it is just as much of an oversimplification to say that adult-imposed values are responsible for the nature of infantile conditioning in any culture. We have a hopelessly vicious circle. Infantile conditioning causes adult personality; adult personality causes infantile conditioning.

What then is the value, if any, of this kind of analysis? I would hope that correlation is worth something, if causation proves to be beyond reach. In other words, I believe there is a correlation, a congruence, an isomorphism, between toilet training in India and the adult behavior as expressed in various manifestations of the pollution complex. This entire essay was devoted to revealing that parallelism in all its complexity.

What is the value of revealing that parallelism? This is the same as asking what is the point of analysis (as opposed to mere description). There is, of course, always the purely intellectual response. Caste and untouchability have puzzled Indologists, anthropologists and others interested in India for centuries. I would like to think that this essay has succeeded, in some measure, in advancing our understanding of caste and untouchability. But there is a possible applied answer to the question as well.

Most of the many individuals who have written on caste and untouchability have not hesitated to place a value judgment on these deeply ingrained aspects of Indian life and culture. Specifically, they have deplored what they consider to be the insidious and demeaning consequences of caste and untouchability, a system that restricts high-ranking castes as well as low-ranking ones. The government of India has tried, unsuccessfully, to wipe out untouchability, for example, but almost all writers have agreed that it is difficult, if not impossible, to legislate it out of existence. If the Gypsy data cited means anything, it shows just how powerful the fear of leftovers, especially feces, really is. One cannot banish such a stratum of cultural coprophobia by decree.

I believe the first step in trying to mitigate, if not eliminate, the devastating impact of untouchability upon millions of individuals—not to mention those yet unborn—is to understand the phenomenon, in all of its manifestations and ramifications. If knowledge isn't power, it can surely lead to power. I am under no illusion that academic treatises like this one are read widely outside of colleges and universities. On the other hand, I would like to think that if there is anything to my overall thesis concerning the underpinning of caste and untouchability, this insight might be of some help in encouraging reformers to take action against forms of caste prejudice and some of the evils of untouchability. For example, if toilet training is truly a partial determining factor for the individual, then one should realize that it is possible to change toilet training techniques. One could encourage mothers to start toilet training later than three months and one could try to minimize the traumatic "crackdown" at age five, for example. But I must leave the problem of what to do about caste and untouchability to those better qualified than I to solve it. Ultimately, it is a problem that Indians are going to have to solve for themselves. If this essay helps them in any way to solve it, I would feel that my time spent in reading Indian ethnography for the past several years has been worthwhile indeed.

# Bibliography

Aarne, Antti, and Stith Thompson. *The Types of the Folktale.* Helsinki: Academia Scientiarum Fennica, 1961.

Acton, Thomas A. "The Functions of the Avoidance of Moxadi Kovels (amongst Gypsies in South Essex)." *Journal of the Gypsy Lore Society* 50 (1971): 108-136.

Aggarwal, Partap C., and Mohd. Siddiq Ashraf. *Equality through Privilege: A Study of Scheduled Castes in Haryana.* New Delhi: Shri Ram Centre, 1976.

Agrawal, Chandra Kumar. "The Comparative Study of Accumulative Drolls of Chhatis Garh." *Folklore* (Calcutta) 3, no. 3 (1962): 126-137.

Alley, Kelly D. "Ganga and Gandagi: Interpretations of Pollution and Waste in Benaras." *Ethnology* 33 (1994): 127-145.

Ambroise, Yvon. "The Hindu Concept of Space and Time Structuring the Day to Day Life of Man." *Social Compass* 29 (1982): 335-348.

Anand, Kulk Raj. *Untouchable.* London: Penguin, 1986.

Anant, Santokh S. "Child Training and Caste Personality: The Need for Further Research." *Race* 8 (1967): 385-394.

Anon. "The Crow and The Sparrow." *North Indian Notes and Queries* 2 (1892): 138.

——. "The Old Woman and the Crow." *North Indian Notes and Queries* 5 (1895): 142.

Appadurai, Arjun. "Right and Left Hand Castes in South India." *The Indian Economic and Social History Review* 11 (1974): 216-259.

Apte, Mahadev L. "'I Am Pure, You Are Polluted!' Who Is Clean and Who Is Dirty? Humor in Ritual Behavior among Marathi Speakers in India." *Etnofoor* 1 (1988): 15-23.

Aung, Maung Htin. *Thirty Burmese Tales*. Calcutta: Oxford University Press, 1952.

Ayyar, P. V. Jagadisa. *South Indian Customs*. New Delhi: Asian Educational Services, 1982.

Bailey, F. C. *Caste and the Economic Frontier*. Manchester, England: Manchester University Press, 1957.

Baker, Sophie. *Caste: At Home in Hindu India*. London: Jonathan Cape, 1990.

Bandyopadhyay, Samaresh. *Early Foreigners on Indian Caste System*. Calcutta: Pilgrim Publishers, 1974.

Banerjee, M.N. "Hindu Family and Freudian Theory." *The Indian Journal of Social Work* 5 (1944-1945): 180-186.

Banerji, Saradindu. "Untouchability." *Samiksa* 34 (1980): 130-133.

Barnett, Steve, Lina Fruzzetti, and Akos Ostor. "Hierarchy Purified: Notes on Dumont and His Critics." *Journal of Asian Studies* 35 (1976): 627-650.

Bassa, D. M. "From the Traditional to the Modern: Some Observations on Changes in Indian Child-Rearing and Parental Attitudes, with Special Reference to Identity Formation." In *The Child in His Family: Children and Parents in a Changing World,* edited by E. James Anthony and Colette Chiland, 333-343. New York: John Wiley, 1978.

Beals, Alan R. *Gopalur: A South Indian Village*. New York: Holt, Rinehart and Winston, 1962.

Bean, Susan S. "Toward A Semiotics of 'Purity' and 'Pollution' in India." *American Ethnologist* 8 (1981): 575-595.

Beck, Brenda E. F. "The Right-Left Division of South Indian Society." In *Right and Left,* edited by Rodney Needham, 391-426. Chicago: University of Chicago Press, 1973.

——. "Frames, Tale Types and Motifs: The Discovery of Indian Oicotypes." In *Indian Folklore II,* edited by Peter J. Claus, Jawaharlal Handoo, and D. P. Pattanayak, 1-43. Mysore, India: Central Institute of Indian Languages, 1987.

Beck, Brenda E. F., and Peter J. Claus, Praphulladatta Goswami, and Jawaharlal Handoo. *Folktales of India*. Chicago: University of Chicago Press, 1987.

Benedict, Ruth. "Continuities and Discontinuities in Cultural Conditioning." *Psychiatry* 1 (1938): 161-167.

——. *Patterns of Culture.* New York: Mentor, 1946.

Berkeley-Hill, Owen. "The Psychology of the Anus." *Indian Medical Gazette* 48 (1913): 301-303.

——. "The Anal-Erotic Factor in the Religion, Philosophy and Character of the Hindus." *International Journal of Psycho-Analysis* 2 (1921): 306-338.

——. *All Too Human: An Unconventional Autobiography.* London: Peter Davies, 1939.

Berreman, Gerald D. "Caste: The Concept of Caste." *International Encyclopedia of the Social Sciences,* Vol. 2 (1968): 333-339. New York: Macmillan & Free Press.

Bhagvat, Durga. "The Sparrow and the Crow." *Indian Folk-Lore* 2 (1959): 213-215.

Blum, Ernst. "Zur Symbolik des Raben." *Psychoanalytische Bewegung* 3 (1931): 359-368.

Blunt, E. A. H. *The Caste System of Northern India.* London: Oxford University Press, 1931.

Bødker, Laurits. *Indian Animal Tales: A Preliminary Survey.* FF Communications No. 170 (1957). Helsinki: Academia Scientiarum Fennica.

——. *Folk Literature (Germanic).* Copenhagen: Rosenkilde and Bagger, 1965.

Bonnerjea, Biren. "Possible Origin of the Caste System in India." *Indian Antiquary* 60 (1931): 49-52; 67-70; 91-95.

Bonos, Arlene Helen. "Roumany Rye of Philadelphia." *American Anthropologist* 44 (1942): 257-274.

Borooah, J. *Folk Tales of Assam.* 2nd ed. Gauhati, India: Lawyer's Book Stall, 1955.

Boss, Medard. *A Psychiatrist Discovers India.* London: Oswald Wolff, 1965.

Briggs, Geo. W. *The Chamars.* Calcutta: Association Press, 1920.

——. *The Doms and Their Near Relations.* Mysore, India: The Wesley Press, 1953.

Brown, W. Norman. "The Sanctity of the Cow in Hinduism." *Journal of the Madras University,* Section A. Humanities 28 (1957): 29-49.

Buck, Carl Darling. *A Dictionary of Selected Synonyms in the Principal*

*Indo-European Languages.* Chicago: University of Chicago Press, 1949.

Bychowski, Gustav. "A Brief Visit to India: Observations and Psychoanalytic Implications." *American Imago* 25 (1968): 59-76.

Carstairs, G. Morris. *The Twice-Born: A Study of a Community of High-Caste Hindus.* London: The Hogarth Press, 1957.

Chakraborty, Ajita, and Gouranga Banerji. "Ritual, A Culture Specific Neurosis, and Obsessional States in Bengali Culture." *Indian Journal of Psychiatry* 17 (1975): 211-216, 273-283.

Chakravarti, Nirmal Kumar. "Origin of Caste (Jati) System in India: A Comprehensive Theory." *Human Science* 38 (1989): 1-13.

Chakravarti, Nirmal Kumar, and Shubhasree Subedi. "Origin of Untouchability in Hinduism." *Man in India* 75 (1995): 139-161.

Charlsley, Simon. "'Untouchable': What Is in a Name?" *Journal of the Royal Anthropological Institute* 2 (1996): 1-23.

Chattopadyay, Kshitishprasad. "The Origin of Castes: A Study of Modern Views." *Visva-Bharati Quarterly* 2 (1924-1925): 347-358.

Cochrane, Timothy. "The Concept of Ecotypes in American Folklore." *Journal of American Folklore* 24 (1987): 33-55.

Cohn, Bernard S. "Notes on the History of the Study of Indian Society and Culture." In *Structure and Change in Indian Society,* edited by Milton Singer and Bernard S. Cohn, 3-28. New York: Wenner-Gren Foundation for Anthropological Research, 1968.

Cowell, E. B. *The Jataka or Studies of the Buddha's Former Births,* Vols. 1-3. London: Routledge & Kegan Paul, 1973.

Crawford, Cromwell. "Ram Mohun Roy on Sati and Sexism." *The Indian Journal of Social Work* 41 (1980): 73-91.

Crooke, W. "The Veneration of the Cow in India." *Folk-Lore* 23 (1912): 275-306.

Currie, Kate. "The Indian Stratification Debate: A Discursive Exposition of Problems and Issues in the Analysis of Class, Caste and Gender." *Dialectical Anthropology* 17 (1992): 115-139.

Dalal, Ajit K., Atul K. Singh, Ambalika Sinha, and Usha Sah. "The Sati of Deorala: An Attributional Study of Social Relations." *The Indian Journal of Social Work* 49 (1988): 349-358.

Damle, Y. B. *Caste—A Review of the Literature on Caste.* Cambridge: Center for International Studies, Massachusetts Institute of Technology, 1961.

Daniel, E. Valentine. *Fluid Signs: Being a Person the Tamil Way.* Berkeley: University of California Press, 1984.

Darling, Malcolm Lyall. *Wisdom and Waste in the Punjab Village.* London: Oxford University Press, 1934.

Das, D. F. *The Untouchable Story.* New Delhi: Allied Publishers Private Limited, 1985.

Das, K. B. and L. K. Mahaptra. *Folk Lore of Orissa.* New Delhi: National Book Trust, 1979.

Das, R. C. "Analysis of a Folk Verse." *Samiksa* 39 (1985): 82-87.

Das, S. K. "A Study of Folk Cattle Rites." *Man in India* 33 (1953): 232-241.

Das, Veena. "The Body as Metaphor." *Manushi* 5(4), no. 28 (1985): 2-6.

Das, Veena, and Jit Singh Uberoi. "The Elementary Structure of Caste." *Contributions to Indian Sociology,* N. S. 5 (1971): 33-43.

Dave, Indu. *Indian Personality in Its Developmental Background.* Udaipur, India: Himanshu Publications, 1991.

Davis, Marvin. "A Philosophy of Hindu Rank from Rural West Bengal." *Journal of Asian Studies* 36 (1976): 5-24.

De Vos, George. "Psychology of Purity and Pollution as Related to Social Self-Identity and Caste." In *Caste and Race: Comparative Approaches,* edited by Anthony de Reuck and Julie Knight, 292-315. Boston: Little, Brown and Company, 1967.

Deliège, Robert. "Les Mythes d'Origine Chez les Paraiyar (Inde du Sud)." *L'Homme* 29 (1989): 107-116.

————. "Replication and Consensus: Untouchability, Caste and Ideology in India." *Man* 27 (1992): 155-173.

Desai, I. P. *Untouchability in Rural Gujurat.* Bombay: Popular Prakashan, 1976.

Deshpande, Shashi. *That Long Silence.* London: Virago Press, 1988.

Devereux, George. "Cultural and Characterological Traits of the Mohave Related to the Anal Stage of Psychological Development." *Psychoanalytic Quarterly* 20 (1951): 398-422.

Digambarji, Swami, and M.I. Gharote. *Gheranda Samhitā.* Lonavla: Kaivalyadhama S. M. Y. M. Samitī, 1978.

Dirks, Nicholas B. "Castes of Mind." *Representations* 37 (Winter 1992): 56-78.

Doniger, Wendy, and Brian K. Smith. *The Laws of Manu.* London:

Penguin, 1991.

Douglas, Mary. *Purity and Danger: An Analysis of Concepts of Pollution and Taboo.* Harmondsworth, England: Penguin, 1970.

Dube, S. C. *Indian Village.* Ithaca, New York: Cornell University Press, 1955.

Dubois, J. A. *Hindu Manners, Customs and Ceremonies.* Oxford: Clarendon Press, 1906.

Dumont, Louis. *Homo Hierarchicus: The Caste System and Its Implications.* Chicago: University of Chicago Press, 1980.

Dundes, Alan. *Life Is Like a Chicken Coop Ladder: A Portrait of German Culture through Folklore.* New York: Columbia University Press, 1984.

———. "Interpreting 'Little Red Riding Hood' Psychoanalytically." In *Little Red Riding Hood: A Casebook,* edited by Alan Dundes, 192-236. Madison: University of Wisconsin Press, 1989.

Dutt, Nripendra Kumar. *Origin and Growth of Caste in India.* 2nd ed. Vol. 1. Calcutta: Firma K.L. Mukhopadyay, 1968.

Eberhard, Wolfram. "The Story of Grandaunt Tiger." In *Little Red Riding Hood: A Casebook,* edited by Alan Dundes, 21-63. Madison: University of Wisconsin Press, 1989.

Edwardes, S. M. "Some Kanarese Proverbs Relating to Caste in Southern India." *Journal of the Anthropological Society of Bombay* 7 (1904-1907): 321-330.

Edwards, James W. "Semen Anxiety in South Asian Cultures: Cultural and Transcultural Significance." *Medical Anthropology* 7, no. 3 (1983): 51-67.

Eggeling, Julius, trans. *The Satapatha-Brâhmana.* 5 Parts. Oxford: Clarendon Press, 1882, 1885, 1894, 1897, 1900.

Eichinger Ferro-Luzzi, Gabriella. "Ritual as Language: The Case of South Indian Food Offerings." *Current Anthropology* 18 (1977): 507-514.

———. *The Self-Milking Cow and the Bleeding Lingam.* Wiesbaden, Germany: Otto Harrassowitz, 1987.

Elwin, Verrier. *Leaves from the Jungle: Life in a Gond Village.* London: John Murray, 1936.

———. *Folk-Tales of Mahakoshal.* Bombay: Oxford University Press, 1944.

Emeneau, M. B. "Studies in the Folktales of India, II: The Old Woman and Her Pig." *Journal of American Folklore* 56 (1943): 272-288.

———. "Kota Texts, Part Two." *University of California Publications in*

*Linguistics* 2, no. 2 (1946): 193-390.

Emerson, Gertrude. *Voiceless India*. Garden City, New Jersey: Doubleday, Doran & Company, 1930.

Ewing, Arthur H. "The Hindu Conception of the Functions of Breath—A Study in Early Hindu Psycho-physics." *Journal of the American Oriental Society* 22, no. 2 (1901): 249-308.

Ficowsky, Jerzy. "Supplementary Notes on the Mageripen Code among Polish Gypsies." *Journal of the Gypsy Lore Society* 30 (1951): 123-132.

Fonesca, Isabel. *Bury Me Standing: The Gypsies and Their Journey*. New York: Alfred A. Knopf, 1995.

Foster, George. "Peasant Society and the Image of Limited Good." *American Anthropologist* 67 (1965): 293-315.

Fraser, Thomas M., Jr. *Culture and Change in India*. Amherst: The University of Massachusetts Press, 1968.

Frazer, James George. *The Magic Art and the Evolution of Kings, Vol. I*. London: Macmillan, 1913.

Freeman, James M. *Untouchable: An Indian Life History*. Stanford: Stanford University Press, 1979.

Frere, Mary. *Old Deccan Days*. London: John Murray, 1868.

Fuchs, Stephen. *The Children of Hari*. Vienna: Verlag Herold, 1950.

——. *At the Bottom of Indian Society: The Harijan and Other Low Castes*. New Delhi: Munshiram Manoharlal Publishers, 1981.

Galanter, Marc. "The Abolition of Disabilities—Untouchability and the Law." In *The Untouchables in Contemporary India,* edited by J. Michael Mahar, 227-314. Tucson: University of Arizona Press, 1972.

Gandhi, M. K. *Gandhi's Autobiography: The Story of My Experiments with Truth*. Washington, DC: Public Affairs Press, 1954a.

——. *The Removal of Untouchability*. Ahmedabad, India: Navajivan Press, 1954b.

——. *Caste Must Go and the Sin of Untouchability*. Ahmedabad, India: Navajivan Press, 1964.

Gandhi, Raj S. "The Caste-Joint Family Axis of Hindu Social System, the Ethnos of Hindu Culture and the Formation of Hindu Personality." *Sociologus* 24 (1974): 56-64.

——. "Sati as Altruistic Suicide." *Contributions to Asian Studies* 10 (1977): 141-157.

——. "The Practice of Untouchability: Persistence and Change." *Humboldt*

*Journal of Social Relations* 10 (1982-1983): 254-275.

Ghurye, G. S. *Caste, Class and Occupation.* Bombay: Popular Book Depot, 1961.

Gilbert, William H. *Caste in India, A Bibliography.* Washington DC, 1948.

Goswami, Praphulladatta. *Tales of Assam.* Gauhati, India: Publication Board, 1990.

Gould, Harold A. *The Hindu Caste System.* Delhi: Chanakya Publications, 1987.

Gough, E. Kathleen. "Letter to the Editor." *Eastern Anthropologist* 10 (1957): 232-234.

Grey, Leslie. *A Concordance of Buddhist Birth Stories.* Oxford: The Pali Text Society, 1990.

Gropper, Rena C. *Gypsies in the City: Culture Patterns and Survival.* Princeton, New Jersey: The Darwin Press, 1975.

Gupta, Nitya N. "Influence of Hindu Culture and Social Customs on Psychosomatic Disease in India." *Psychosomatic Medicine* 18 (1956): 506-510.

Haavio, Martti. *Kettenmärchen-Studien II.* FF Communications No. 99. Helskinki: Academia Scientiarum Fennica, 1932.

Hamilton, Ian. "The First Life of Salman Rushdie." *The New Yorker* 71, no. 42 (1996): 90-113.

Hand, Wayland. "The Magical Transference of Disease." In *Folklore Studies in Honor of Arthur Palmer Hudson,* edited by Daniel W. Patterson, 83-109. Chapel Hill: The North Carolina Folklore Society, 1965.

Hanumanthan, K. R. *Untouchability: A Historical Study up to 1500 A.D.* Madurai, India: Koodal Publishers, 1979.

Harper, Edward B. "Ritual Pollution as an integrator of Caste and Religion." In *Religion in South Asia,* edited by Edward B. Harper, 151-196. Seattle: University of Washington Press, 1964.

Harris, Marvin. "The Myth of the Sacred Cow." In *Man, Culture, and Animals,* edited by Anthony Leeds and Andrew P. Vayda, 217-222. Washington, DC: American Association for the Advancement of Science, 1965.

____. "India's Sacred Cow." *Human Nature* 1, no. 2 (1978): 28-36.

Hartnack, Christiane. "British Psychoanalysts in Colonial India." In *Psychology in Twentieth-Century Thought and Society,* edited by Mitchell G. Ash and William R. Woodward, 233-251.

Cambridge: Cambridge University Press, 1987.

Hazari. *Indian Outcaste: The Autobiography of an Untouchable.* London: The Bannisdale Press, 1951.

Hershman, Paul. "Hair, Sex, and Dirt." *Man* 9 (1974): 274-298.

———. "Virgin and Mother." In *Symbols and Sentiments,* edited by Ioan Lewis, 269-292. London: Academic Press, 1977.

Hertel, Johannes. "Über einen südlichen *textus amplior* des Panchatantra." *Zeitschrift der Deutschen Morgenländischen Gesellschaft* 60 (1906): 769-801; 61 (1907): 18-72.

Hill, Charles. "Origin of the Caste System in India." *Indian Antiquary* 59 (1930): 51-54, 72-75, 81-84, 195-197.

Hitchcock, John T. *The Magars of Banyan Hill.* New York: Holt, Rinehart and Winston, 1966.

Hocart, A. M. *Caste: A Comparative Study.* New York: Russel & Russel, 1968.

Hockings, Paul. "The Abbé Dubois, an Early French Ethnographer." *Contributions to Indian Sociology* 11 (1977): 329-343.

Hodgen, Margaret T. "Geographical Diffusion as a Criterion of Age." *American Anthropologist* 44 (1942): 345-367.

Honko, Lauri. "The Formation of Oicotypes." In *Folklore on Two Continents: Essays in Honor of Linda Dégh,* edited by Nikolai Burlakoff and Carl Lindahl, 280-285. Bloomington, Indiana: Trickster Press, 1980.

Hultkrantz, Åke. *General Ethnological Concepts.* Copenhagen: Rosenkilde and Bagger, 1960.

Hutton, J.H. *Caste in India: Its Nature, Function, and Origins.* 4th ed., Bombay: Oxford University Press, 1963.

Ikeda, Hiroko. *A Type and Motif Index of Japanese Folk-Literature.* FF Communications No. 209. Helsinki: Academia Scientiarium Fennica, 1971.

Inden, Ronald. "Orientalist Constructions of India." *Modern Asian Studies* 20 (1986): 401-446.

Isaacs, Harold R. *India's Ex-Untouchables.* New York: The John Day Company, 1965.

Islam, Mazharul. *A History of Folktale Collections in India and Pakistan.* Dacca, Bangladesh: Bengali Academy, 1970.

Jaiswal, Sushma, and Hirdaipal Grewal. "Child Rearing Practices in India." *Indian Psychological Review* 33, no. 6-7 (1988): 30-40.

James, P. A. and G. Sreenivas Reddy. "Anti-Untouchability Legislation in India." *Journal of Administration Overseas* 19 (1980): 112-116.

Jasimuddin. *Folk Tales of Bangladesh.* Dacca, Bangladesh: Oxford University Press, 1967.

Jensen, Herman. *A Classified Collection of Tamil Proverbs.* New Delhi: Asian Educational Services, 1986.

Jha, Vivekanand. "Stages in the History of Untouchables." *Indian Historical Review* 2 (1975): 14-31.

Jones, Ernest. "The Madonna's Conception through the Ear." In *Essays in Applied Psychoanalysis, Vol. II,* 266-357. London: Hogarth Press, 1951.

——. "Anal-Erotic Character Traits." In *Papers on Psycho-Analysis,* 413-437. Boston: Beacon Press, 1961.

Kadetotad, N. K. "Caste Hierarchy among the Untouchables of Dharwar." *Eastern Anthropologist* 19 (1966): 205-214.

Kakar, Sudhir. *The Inner World: A Psycho-Analytic Study of Childhood and Society in India,* 2nd ed. Delhi: Oxford University Press, 1981.

Kamaraju, Malyala S. S., and K. V. Ramana. "Untouchability—The Need for a New Approach." *The Indian Journal of Social Work* 45 (1984): 361-369.

Kamble, N. D. *The Scheduled Castes.* New Delhi: Ashish Publishing House, 1982.

Kane, Pandurang Vaman. *History of Dharmasāstra, Vol. II, Part I,* 2nd ed. Poona: Shandarkar Oriental Research Institute, 1974.

Kaushik, Meena. "The Symbolic Representation of Death." *Contributions to Indian Sociology,* N. S. 10 (1976): 265-292.

Kapani, Lakshmi, and François Chenet. "India and the Risk of Psychoanalysis." *Diogenes* 135 (1986): 63-78.

Karve, Irawati. "What is Caste?" *Economic Weekly* 10 (1958): 125-138, 401-407, 881-888; 11 (1959): 149-163.

——. "On the Road: A Maharashtrian Pilgrimage." *Journal of Asian Studies* 22 (1962): 13-29.

Kearns, James F. "The Right-Hand and the Left-Hand Castes." *Indian Antiquary* 5 (1876): 353-354.

Ketkar, S. V. *History of Caste in India.* Jaipur: Rawat Publications, 1979.

Khan, Mumtaz Ali. *Scheduled Castes and Their Status in India.* New Delhi: Uppal Publishing House, 1980.

Khare, R. S. "Ritual Purity and Pollution in Relation to Domestic Sanitation." *Western Anthropologist* 15 (1962): 125-139.

———. *The Hindu Hearth and Home.* Durham: Carolina Academic Press, 1976a.

———. "'Right' and 'Left' in Indian Society." *Man* 11 (1976b): 438-439.

———. "The One and the Many: Varna and Jati as a Symbolic Classiication." In *American Studies in the Anthropology of India,* edited by Sylvia Vatuk, 35-61. New Delhi: Manohar, 1978.

Kirfel, Willibald. *Die fünf Elemente insbesondere Wasser und Feuer, ihre Bedeutung für den Ursprung altindischer und altmediterraner Heilkunde. Eine medizingeschichtliche Studie.* Walldorf-Hessen: Verlag für Orientkunde, 1951.

Kishwar, Madhu, and Ruth Vanita. "The Burning of Roop Kanwar." *Manushi* 42-43 (1987): 15-25.

Klass, Morton. *Caste: The Emergence of the South Asian Social System.* Philadelphia: Institute for the Study of Human Issues, 1980.

Kochar, V. K., G. A. Schad, A. B. Chowdhury, C. G. Dean, and T. Nawalinski. "Human Factors in the Regulation of Parasitic Infections: Cultural Ecology of Hookworm Populations in Rural West Bengal." In *Medical Anthropology,* edited by Francis X. Grollig and Harold B. Haley, 287-312. The Hague, Netherlands: Mouton, 1976.

Koestler, Arthur. *The Lotus and the Robot.* New York: The Macmillan Company, 1961.

Kolenda, Pauline. *Caste in Contemporary India: Beyond Organic Solidarity.* Menlo Park, California: The Benjamin/Cummings Publishing Company, 1978.

Kothari, Rajni. *Politics in India.* Boston: Little, Brown and Company, 1970.

Kready, Laura F. *A Study of Fairy Tales.* Boston: Houghton Mifflin, 1916.

Kripal, Jeffrey J. *Kali's Child.* Chicago: University of Chicago Press, 1995.

Kristeva, Julia. *Powers of Horror: An Essay on Abjection.* New York: Columbia University Press, 1982.

Kroeber, A. L. "Caste." *Encyclopedia of the Social Sciences, Vol. III.* New York: Macmillan, 1930, 254-257.

Kshirsagar, R. K. *Untouchability in India.* New Delhi: Deep and Deep Publications, 1986.

Kubie, Lawrence S. "The Fantasy of Dirt." *Psychoanalytic Quarterly* 6 (1937): 388-425.

Kulkarni, Manu N. "Right to defecate." *Manushi* 83 (July-August 1994): 22-23.

Kundu, Nityananda. "Social Distance Observed in a Maharashtra Village." *Journal of the Indian Anthropological Society* 17 (1983): 269-274.

Kurtz, Stanley N. *All the Mothers Are One: Hindu India and the Cultural Reshaping of Psychoanalysis.* New York: Columbia University Press, 1992.

Lal, Hira. "Untouchables amongst Animals and Plants." *Man in India* 7 (1927): 337-338.

Lal, Sheo Kumar, and Umed Raj Najar. *Extent of Untouchability and Pattern of Discrimination.* New Delhi: Mittal Publications, 1990.

Lambert, R. D. "Untouchability as a Social Problem: Theory and Research." *Sociological Bulletin* 7 (1958): 55-61.

Landauer, Karl. "Some Remarks on the Formation of Anal-Erotic Character." *International Journal of Psycho-Analysis* 20 (1939): 418-423.

Lannoy, Richard. *The Speaking Tree: A Study of Indian Culture and Society.* New York: Oxford University Press, 1971.

Lee, Ronald. "The Gypsies in Canada: An Ethnological Study." *Journal of the Gypsy Lore Society,* 3rd series, 46 (1967): 38-51; 47 (1968): 12-28; 48 (1969): 92-107.

———. *Goddam Gypsy: An Autobiographical Novel.* Indianapolis: Bobbs-Merrill, 1972.

Lewis, Christopher Alan. "The Anal-Erotic Factor in Hindus and Muslims: An Empirical Examination of Berkeley-Hill's Hypothesis." *Psychological Reports* 71 (1992): 643-648.

*Lilacaritra. Sri Cakradjara Lilacaritra.* Mumbai, India: Maharashtra Rajya Sahitya-Saskrti Mandala, 1982.

Lincoln, Bruce. "The Indo-European Myth of Creation." *History of Religions* 15 (1975): 121-145.

Linton, Ralph. *The Study of Man.* New York: Appleton-Century-Crofts, 1936.

Lodrick, Deryck O. *Sacred Cows, Sacred Places: Origins and Survivals of Animal Homes in India.* Berkeley: University of California Press, 1981.

Madan, T. W. "Review of *Village India.*" *Eastern Anthropologist* 9

(1955): 129-135.

Malamoud, Charles. "Observations sur la Notion de 'Reste' dans le Brahmanisme." *Wiener Zeitschrift für de Kunde Südasiens* 16 (1972): 5-26.

Malkani, N. R. *Clean People and an Unclean Country.* New Delhi: Harijan Sevak Sangh, 1965.

Mandelbaum, David G. "Concepts and Methods in the Study of Caste." *Economic Weekly* 11 (1959): 145-148.

Mann, Stuart E. *An Indo-European Comparative Dictionary.* Hamburg: Helmut Buske Verlag, 1984.

Marfatia, J. C. "Bedwetting—Its Causes and Treatment." *The Indian Journal of Social Work* 4 (1943-1944): 301-313.

Marglin, Frederique Apffel. "Power, Purity and Pollution: Aspects of the Caste System Reconsidered." *Contributions to Indian Sociology* 2 (1977): 245-270.

Margul, Tadeusz. "Present Day Worship of the Cow in India." *Numen* 15 (1968): 63-80.

Marriott, McKim. "Interactional and Attributional Theories of Caste Ranking." *Man* 39 (1959): 92-107.

——. "Caste Ranking and Food Transactions: A Matric Analysis." In *Structure and Change in Indian Society,* edited by Milton Singer and Bernard S. Cohn, 133-171. Viking Fund Publications in Anthropology 47, Foundation for Anthropological Research. New York: Wenner-Gren, 1968.

Mayer, Adrian C. "Some Hierarchical Aspects of Caste." *Southwestern Journal of Anthropology* 12 (1956): 117-144.

Mayo, Katherine. *Mother India.* London: Jonathan Cape, 1932.

Mazumdar, Vina. "Comment on Suttee." *Signs* 4 (1978): 269-273.

Mencher, Joan. "Growing Up in South Malabar." *Human Organization* 22 (1963): 54-65.

Miller, Carol. "American Rom and the Ideology of Defilement." In *Gypsies, Tinkers and Other Travellers,* edited by Farnham Rehfisch, 41-54. London: Academic Press, 1975.

Milner, Murray, Jr. "Dirt and Development in India." *Virginia Quarterly Review* 63 (1987): 54-71.

——. "Hindu Eschatology and the Indian Caste System: An Example of Structural Reversal." *Journal of Asian Studies* 52 (1993): 298-319.

——. *Status and Sacredness: A General Theory of Status Relations and an*

*Analysis of Indian Culture.* New York: Oxford University Press, 1994.

Minturn, Leigh, and John T. Hitchcock. *The Rajputs of Khalapur, India.* New York: John Wiley, 1966.

Misra, P. K. "Persistence of Untouchability: Analysis of Two Case Studies in a Multi-Ethnic Area of Orissa." *Manav* 1, no. 1 (1982-1983): 124-137.

Mitra, Sarat Chandra. "On Some Superstitions Prevalent in Bengal." *Journal of the Anthropological Society of Bombay* 2 (1889-1892): 582-596.

———. "Bengali and Behari Folk-Lore about Birds, Part 1." *Journal of the Asiatic Society of Bengal* 67, no. 3 (1898): 67-74.

———. "An Accumulation Droll and Rhyme from Bihar, with Remarks on Accumulation Drolls." *Journal of the Asiatic Society of Bengal* 70 (1903): 99-104.

———. "Studies in Bird Myths No. XI—On An Aetiological Myth about the Indian House-Crow." *Quarterly Journal of the Mythic Society* 17 (1926-1927): 143-144.

———. "On Two Accumulation Drolls of 'The Prawn and the Crow Type'." *Journal of the Department of Letters* (University of Calcutta) 14, no. 6 (1927): 1-18.

Moffatt, Michael. *An Untouchable Community in South India: Structure and Consensus.* Princeton, New Jersey: Princeton University Press, 1979.

Mohapatra, Kulamoni, and A. D. Mohanty. "Study of the Problem of Untouchability." *Adibasi* 15 (1973-1974): 18-27.

Moudgil, Ranvir. "Child Rearing Practices and Hindu Personality Formation." *International Journal of Social Psychiatry* 18 (1972): 127-131.

Muecke, Marjorie A. "An Explication of 'Wind Illness' in Northern Thailand." *Culture, Medicine and Psychiatry* 3 (1979): 267-300.

Muehl, John Frederick. *Interview with India.* New York: The John Day Company, 1950.

Muensterberger, Warner. "Psyche and Environment: Sociocultural Variations in Separation and Individuation." *Psychoanalytic Quarterly* 38 (1969): 191-216.

Murdoch, J. *Review of Caste in India.* Jaipur, India: Rawat Publications, 1977.

Murphy, Lois Barclay. "Roots of Tolerance and Tensions in Indian

Child Development." In *In the Minds of Men: The Study of Human Behavior and Social Tensions in India,* edited by Gardner Murphy, 46-58. New York: Basic Books, 1953.

Nadel, S. F. "Caste and Government in Primitive Society." *Journal of the Anthropological Society of Bombay* 8, no. 2 (1954): 9-22.

Nagendra, S. P. "The Traditional Theory of Caste." In *Towards a Sociology of Culture in India,* edited by T. K. N. Unnithan, Indra Deva and Yogendra Singh, 262-273. New Delhi: Prentice Hall of India, 1965.

Naipal, V. S. *An Area of Darkness.* London: Andre Deutsch, 1964.

——. *India: A Wounded Civilization.* New York: Alfred A. Knopf, 1977.

——. *India: A Million Mutinies Now.* New York: Viking, 1991.

Nair, K. N. "Animal Protein Consumption and the Sacred Cow Complex in India." In *Food and Evolution: Toward a Theory of Human Food Habits,* edited by Marvin Harris and Eric B. Ross, 445-454. Philadelphia: Temple University Press, 1987.

Nandy, Ashis. "Sati: A Nineteenth Century Tale of Women, Violence and Protest." In *At The Edge of Psychology*, 1-31. Delhi: Oxford University Press, 1980.

Nandy, Ashis, and Sudhir Kakar. "Culture and Personality." In *A Survey of Research in Psychology, 1971-1976,* edited by Udai Pareek, 136-167. Bombay: Popular Prakashan, 1980.

Narain, Dhirendra. *Hindu Character (A Few Glimpses).* Bombay: Bombay University Press, 1957.

——. "Growing up in India." *Family Process* 3 (1964):127-154.

Narasimhan, Sakuntala. *Sati: Widow Burning in India.* New York: Doubleday Anchor, 1992.

Neki, J. S. "Psychology in India: Past, Present, and Future." *American Journal of Psychotherapy* 29 (1975): 92-100.

Nettl, Bruno. "The Hymns of the Amish: An Example of Marginal Survival." *Journal of American Folklore* 70 (1957): 323-328.

Obeyesekere, Gananath. "The Left-Right Subcastes in South India: A Critique." *Man* 10 (1975): 462-468.

O'Flaherty, Wendy Doniger. *The Origins of Evil in Hindu Mythology.* Berkeley: University of California Press, 1976.

——. *The Rig Veda.* Harmondsworth, England: Penguin, 1981.

O'Keefe, Daniel Lawrence. *Stolen Lightening: The Social Theory of Magic.* New York: Vintage Books, 1983.

Okely, Judith. "Gypsy Women: Models in Conflict." In *Percieving*

*Women,* edited by Shirley Ardener, 55-86. New York: John Wiley & Sons, 1975.

———. *The Traveller-Gypsies.* Cambridge: Cambridge University Press, 1983a.

———. "Why Gypsies Hate Cats But Love Horses." *New Society* 63 (1983b): 251-253.

Oldenberg, Hermann. "On the History of the Indian Caste-System." *Indian Antiquary* 49 (1920): 205-214, 224-231.

O'Malley, L. S. S. *Indian Caste Customs.* Cambridge: Cambridge University Press, 1932.

Orenstein, Henry. "Toward a Grammar of Defilement in Hindu Sacred Law." In *Structure and Change in Indian Society,* edited by Milton Singer and Bernard S. Cohn, 115-131. Viking Fund Publications in Anthropology 47. New York: Wenner-Gren Foundation for Anthropological Research, 1968.

Pandey, Rajendra. *The Caste System in India: Myth and Reality.* New Delhi: Criterion Publications, 1986.

Parry, Jonathan. "Death and Digestion: The Symbolism of Food and Eating in North Indian Mortuary Rites." *Man* 20 (1985): 612-630.

Parui, Sasanka Sekhar. "Untouchability in the Early Indian Society." *Journal of Indian History* 39 (1961): 1-11.

Passin, Herbert. "Untouchability in the Far East." *Monumenta Nipponica* 11 (1955): 247-267.

Patell, Khan Bahadur Bomanjee Byramjee. "A Few Dreams and Their Interpretations among the Natives of Bombay." *Journal of the Anthropological Society of Bonbay* 7 (1904-1907): 135-147.

Pitt-Rivers, Julian. "On the Word 'Caste'." In *The Translation of Culture: Essays to E. E. Evans-Pritchard,* edited by T. O. Beidelman, 231-256. London: Tavistock Publications, 1971.

Pocock, David F. "Psychological Approaches and Judgements of Reality." *Contributions to Indian Sociology* 5 (1961): 44-74.

Pohlman, Edward W. "Evidences of Disparity between the Hindu Practice of Caste and the Ideal Type." *American Sociological Review* 16 (1951): 375-379.

Polo, Marco. *The Travels of Marco Polo.* New York: Dell, 1961.

Quigley, Declan. *The Interpretation of Caste.* Oxford: Clarendon Press, 1993.

Raheja, Gloria Goodwin. "India: Caste, Kingship, and Dominance

Reconsidered." *Annual Review of Anthropology* 17 (1988a): 497-522.

——. *The Poison in the Gift.* Chicago: University of Chicago Press, 1988b.

Rajan, K. V. "Man, Society and Nation—A Psychoanalyst's View." In *Human Person, Society and State,* edited by P. D. Devanandan & M. N. Thomas, 34-55. Bangalore, India: The Committee for Literature on Social Concerns, 1957.

Ram, L. L. Sundara. "The Sanctity of the Cow in India." *The Quarterly Journal of the Mythic Society* 17 (1926-1927): 277-293.

Ramana, C. V. "On the Early History and Development of Psychoanalysis in India." *Journal of the American Psychoanalytic Association* 12 (1964): 110-134.

Ramanujam, B. K. "Implications of Some Psychoanalytic Concepts in the Indian Context." In *Psychoanalytic Anthropology after Freud,* edited by David H. Spain, 121-135. New York: Psyche Press, 1992.

Ramanujan, A. K. "An Indian Oedipus." In *Oedipus: A Folklore Casebook,* edited by Lowell Edmunds and Alan Dundes, 234-261. New York: Garland, 1983.

——. "The Relevance of South Asian Folklore." In *Indian Folklore II,* edited by Peter J. Claus, Jawaharlal Handoo, and D. P. Pattanayak, 79-116. Mysore, India: Central Institute of Indian Languages, 1987.

——. "Telling Tales." *Daedalus* 118, no. 4 (1989): 239-261.

——. *A Flowering Tree and Other Oral Tales from India.* Berkeley: University of Caliornia Press, 1997.

Ramasamy, Rajakrishnan. *Caste Consciousness among Indian Tamils in Malaysia.* Petaling Jaya, Selangor, Malaysia: Pelanduk Publications, 1984.

Ramu, G. N. "Untouchability in Rural Areas." *The Indian Journal of Social Work* 29 (1968): 147-155.

Randeria, Shalini. "Death and Defilement: Divergent Accounts of Untouchability in Gujarat." In *Rites and Beliefs in Modern India,* edited by Gabriella Eichinger Ferro-Luzzi, 35-51. New Delhi: Manohar, 1990.

Rao, A. Venkoba. "Psychiatric Thought in Ancient India." *Indian Journal of Psychiatry* 20 (1978): 107-119.

Rao, Aparna. "Some Manus Concepts and Attitudes." In *Gypsies, Tinkers and Other Travellers,* edited by Farnham Rehfisch, 139-

167. London: Academic Press, 1975.

Rao, C. Hayavadana. "Indian Nursery Rhymes." *The Quarterly Journal of the Mythic Society* 16 (1925-1926): 31-35.

Rao, R. Sangeetha. *Caste System in India: Myth and Reality.* New Delhi: Indian Publishers, 1989.

Raychaudhuri, Upendrakishore. *The Stupid Tiger and Other Tales.* London: Andre Deutch, 1981.

Rueck, Anthony de, and Julie Knight, eds. *Caste and Race: Comparative Approaches.* Boston: Little, Brown and Company, 1967.

Roberts, Warren E. "A Spaniolic-Jewish Version of 'Frau Holle'." In *Studies in Jewish Biblical Folklore,* edited by Raphael Patai, Francis Lee Utley, and Dov Noy, 177-182. Bloomington: Indiana University Press, 1960.

Robertson, Alexander. *The Mahar Folk: A Study of Untouchables in Maharastra.* Calcutta: Y. M. C. A. Publishing House, 1938.

Rodhe, Sten. *Deliver Us from Evil: Studies on the Vedic Ideas of Salvation.* Lund, Sweden: C. S. K. Gleerup, 1946.

Róheim, Géza. "Wedding Ceremonies in European Folklore." *Samiksa* 8 (1954): 137-173.

Roland, Alan. "Psychoanalytic Perspectives on Personality Development in India." *International Review of Psycho-Analysis* 7 (1980): 73-87.

———. "Toward a Psychoanalytical Psychology of Hierarchical Relationships in Hindu India." *Ethos* 10 (1982): 232-253.

———. *In Search of Self in India and Japan: Toward A Cross Cultural Psychology.* Princeton, New Jersey: Princeton University Press, 1988.

Roy, Prodipto. "The Sacred Cow in India." *Rural Sociology* 20 (1958): 8-15.

Roy, S. C. "Caste, Race, and Religion in India." *Man in India* 14 (1934): 39-63, 75-220, 271-311.

Roy, Satindra Narayan. "The Indian Crow." *Journal of the Anthro pological Society of Bombay* 14 (1927-1931): 525-535.

Rushdie, Salman. *Midnight's Children.* New York: Avon Books, 1982.

Sagar, Sunder Lal. *Hindu Culture and Caste System in India.* Delhi: Uppal Book Store, 1975.

Sakya, Karna, and Linda Griffith. *Tales of Kathmandu: Folktales from the Himalayan Kingdom of Nepal.* Kathmandu, Nepal: House of Kathmandu, 1980.

San Roman, Teresa. "Kinship, Marriage, Law and Leadership in Two Urban Gypsy Settlements in Spain." In *Gypsies, Tinkers and Other Travellers,* edited by Farnham Rehfisch, 161-175. London: Academic Press, 1975.

Saraf, Samarendra. "The Hindu Ritual Purity-Pollution Complex." *Eastern Anthropologist* 22 (1969): 161-175.

____. "Ritual Purity-Pollution Theme: An Analytical Study." *Journal of Social Research* 14, no. 2 (1971): 14-22.

Saraswati, Baidyanath. "Untouchability in Hindu Society: An Interpretation." *Journal of Social Research* 30 (1987):12-22.

Schermerhorn, R. A. "The Indian Constitution and the Untouchability Offences Act." *Indian Journal of Politics* 9 (1975): 13-19.

Schwartz, Barton M., ed. *Caste in Overseas Indian Communities.* San Francisco: Chandler Publishing Company, 1967.

Scott, T. J. "The Knights of the Broom." *Missionary Review of the World* 21 (1898): 256-261.

Searle-Chatterjee, Mary. "The Polluted Identity of Work: A Study of Benares Sweepers." In *Social Anthropology of Work,* edited by Sandra Wallman, A. S. A., 259-286. Monograph 19. London: Academic Press, 1979.

Sekine, Yasumasa. *Theories of Pollution: Theoretical Perspective and Practice in a South Indian Tamil Village.* Monumenta Serindica No. 21. Tokyo: Institute for the Study of Languages and Cultures of Asia and Africa, 1989.

Sengupta, Sankar. *Folklorists of Bengal.* Calcutta: Indian Publications, 1965.

____. "Two Folktales of Bengal." *Folklore* (Calcutta) 32 (1991): 193-198.

Sharma, Arvind. "The Caste System: A Documentary Examination." *The Australian Journal of Politics and History* 35 (1989): 396-406.

Sharma, Girdhar Behari. "Enforcement of the Untouchability Offences Act in India." *Political Science Review* 13 (1974): 305-326.

Sharma, Mohan Lal. "The Myth of the Sacred Cow." *Journal of Popular Culture* 2 (1968): 457-467.

Sharma, S. S. "Untouchability: A Myth or a Reality." *Sociological Bulletin* 35 (1986): 68-79.

Sharma, Satya P. "A Materialist Thesis on the Origin and Continuity of the Caste System in South Asia," *Eastern Anthropologist* 36 (1983): 55-77.

Sharrock, John A. *South Indian Missions.* Westminster, England: Society for the Propagation of the Gospel in Foreign Parts, 1910.

Sheorey, Indumati. *Folk Tales of Maharashtra.* New Delhi: Sterling Publishers, 1973.

Sheth, Surabhi. "Origins of Untouchability in India." *The Indian Journal of Social Science* 3 (1990): 589-596.

Shrivastava, Sushila. "Techniques of Toilet Training During Infancy and Their Effects on Certain Behaviour in Childhood." *Indian Psychological Review* 33, nos. 10-12. (1988): 38-46.

Shukla, Shrilal. *Raagdarbari: A Novel.* New Delhi: Penguin Books, 1992.

Siddiqui, Ashraf. *Toontoony and Other Stories.* Dacca, Bangladesh: University Press Limited, 1980.

Silvan, M. "Reply to Alan Roland's Paper on 'Psychoanalytic Perspectives on Personality Development in India'." *International Review of Psychoanalysis* 8 (1981): 93-99.

Silverman, Carol. "Strategies of Ethnic Adaptation: The Case of Gypsies in the United States." In *Creative Ethnicity,* edited by Stephen Stern and John Allan Cicala, 107-121. Logan: Utah State University Press, 1991.

Simoons, Frederick J. "The Purificatory Role of the Five Products of the Cow in Hinduism." *Ecology of Food and Nutrition* 3 (1974): 21-34.

_____. "Questions in the Sacred Cow Controversy." *Current Anthropology* 20 (1979): 467-493.

Singh, Saint Nihal. "India's 'Untouchables'." *The Contemporary Review* 103 (1913): 376-385.

Singh, T. R. "Some Aspects of Ritual Purity and Pollution." *Eastern Anthropologist* 19 (1966): 131-142.

Sinha, Durganand. "Caste Dynamics: A Psychological Analysis." *Eastern Anthropologist* 12 (1960): 159-171.

_____. *Psychology in a Third World Community: The Indian Experience.* New Delhi: Sage Publications, 1986.

Sinha, T. C. "Development of Psycho-Analysis in India." *International Journal of Psychoanalysis* 47 (1966): 427-439.

_____. "Psychoanalysis and the Family in India." *Samiksa* 31 (1977): 95-105.

Slater, Philip. *The Glory of Hera: Greek Mythology and the Greek Family.* Boston: Beacon Press, 1968.

Smith, Brian K. "Classifying the Universe: Ancient Indian Cosmogonies and the Varna System." *Contributions to Indian Sociology* 23 (1989): 241-260.

Sorabji, Cornelia. *Between the Twilights: Being Studies of Indian Women by One of Themselves.* London: Harper and Brothers, 1908.

——. "Temple-Entry and Untouchability." *The Nineteenth Century* 113 (1933): 689-702.

Spellman, John W. *The Beautiful Blue Jay and Other Tales of India.* Boston: Little, Brown and Company, 1967.

Spratt, P. *Hindu Culture and Personality: A Psycho-Analytic Study.* Bombay: Manaktalas, 1966.

Srinivas, M. N. *Religion and Society among the Coorgs of South India.* Bombay: Media Promoters and Publishers, 1952.

——. "The Caste of the Potter and the Priest." *Man in India* 39 (1959): 190-209.

——. *Caste in Modern Indian and Other Essays.* New York: Asia Publishing House, 1962.

——. *The Remembered Village.* Berkeley: University of California Press, 1976.

——. "Some Reflections on the Nature of Caste Hierarchy." *Contributions to Indian Sociology* 18 (1984): 151-167.

Srinivas, M. N., Y. M. Damle, S. Shahan, and André Béteille. "Caste: A Trend Report and Bibliography." *Current Sociology* 8 (1959): 135-183.

Srinivas, M. N., and André Béteille. "The 'Untouchables' of India." *Scientific American* 213, no. 6 (1965): 13-17.

Srinivasachari, C. S. "The Origin of the Right and Left Hand Castes Divisions." *Journal of the Andhra Historical Research Society* 4 (1930):77-85.

Srinivasan, Doris. *Concept of Cow in the Rigveda.* Delhi: Motilal Banarsidass, 1979.

Steel, Flora Annie. *Tales of the Panjab Told by the People.* London: Macmillan, 1894.

Steel, F. A., and R. C. Temple. "Folklore in the Panjab." *Indian Antiquary* 9 (1880): 205-210, 280-282, 302-304.

Stein, Dorothy K. "Women to Burn: Suttee as a Normative Institution." *Signs* 4 (1978): 253-268.

Stevenson, H. N. C. "Status Evaluation in the Hindu Caste System." *Journal of the Royal Anthropological Institute* 84 (1954): 45-65.

Stevenson, Sinclair, Mrs. *The Rites of the Twice-Born.* London: Oxord University Press, 1920.

——. *Without the Pale: The Life Story of an Outcaste.* Calcutta: Association Press, 1930.

Straus, Murray A. "Anal and Oral Frustration in Relation to Sinhalese Personality." *Sociometry* 20 (1957):21-31.

Sutherland, Anne. *Gypsies: The Hidden Americans.* New York: The Free Press, 1975.

——. "The Body as a Social Symbol among the Rom." In *The Anthropology of the Body,* edited by John Blacking. A. S. A., 375-390. Monograph 15. London: Academic Press, 1977.

Tagore, R. "The Cleanser." *The Visva-Bharati Quarterly* 3 (1925): 148.

Taylor, Susette M. "Indian Folktales." *Folk-Lore* 6 (1895): 399-406; 7 (1896): 83-88.

Taylor, William Stephens. "Basic Personality in Orthodox Hindu Culture Patterns." *Journal of Abnormal and Social Psychology* 43 (1948): 3-12.

Thakkar, K. K. "The Problem of Casteeism and Untouchability." *The Indian Journal of Social Work* 17 (1956): 44-49.

Thaliath, Joseph. "Notes on the Scavenger Caste of Northern Madhya Pradesh, India." *Anthropos* 56 (1961): 789-817.

Thompson, Stith. *Motif-Index of Folk-Literature.* 6 vols. Bloomington: Indiana University Press, 1955-1958.

Thompson, Stith, and Jonas Balys. *The Oral Tales of India.* Bloomington: Indiana University Press, 1958.

Thompson, Thomas William. "The Uncleanness of Women among English Gypsies." *Journal of the Gypsy Lore Society,* 3rd series, 1 (1922): 15-43.

——. "Additional Notes on English Gypsy Uncleanness Taboos." *Journal of the Gypsy Lore Society,* 3rd series, 8 (1929): 33-39.

Ting, Nai-tung. *A Type Index of Chinese Folktales.* FF Communications No. 223. Helsinki: Academia Scientiarum Fennica, 1978.

Tong, Diane. *Gypsies: A Multidisciplinary Annotated Bibliography.* New York: Garland, 1995.

Upadhyaya, Hari S. "History of Folktale Scholarship in India from 1873 to 1962." *Journal of the Ohio Folklore Society* 3 (1968): 227-242.

Upadhyaya, K. D. "A General Survey of Indian Folk-Tales." *Internationaler Kongress der Volkserzahlungsforscher in Kiel und*

*Kopenhagen,* 432-445. Berlin: Walter De Gruyter, 1961.

Vasu, Sivachandra. *The Hindoos as They Are.* 2nd ed. Calcutta: Thacker, Spink and Co., 1883.

Vatuk, Ved Prakash. "Let's Dig Up Some Dirt: The Idea of Humor in Children's Folklore in India." In *VIIIth Congress of Anthropological and Ethnological Sciences, Vol. II,* 274-277. Tokyo: Science Council of Japan, 1970.

Venkataswami, M. N. *Heeramma and Jenkataswami or Folktales from India.* Madras: Diocesan Press, 1923.

Viljanen-Saira, Anna Maria. "The Dimensions of Hierarchy within the Gypsy Culture: An Analysis of the Spatial Regulations Concerning Two-Wheel Carts and Living Accomodations." In *Congressus Quintus Internationalis Fenno-Ugristarum, Part IV,* edited by Osmo Ikola, 217-226. Turku, Finland: Suomen Kielen Seura.

Weber, Max. *The Religion of India.* Glencoe, IL: The Free Press, 1958.

Wesselski, Albert. "Das Märlein von dem Tode des Hühnchens und andere Kettenmärlein." *Hessische Blätter für Volkskunde* 32 (1933): 1-51.

Weyrauch, Walter Otto, and Maureen Anne Bell. "Autonomous Law making: The Case of the 'Gypsies'." *The Yale Law Journal* 103 (1993): 323-399.

Whiting, John W. M., and Irvin L. Child. *Child Training and Personality: A Cross-Cultural Study.* New Haven, CT: Yale University Press, 1953.

Whyte, Betsy. *The Yellow on the Broom.* Edinburgh: Chambers, 1979.

Wiser, William H., and Charlotte Viall Wiser. *Behind Mud Walls, 1930-1960.* Berkeley: University of California Press, 1971.

Wolpert, Stanley. *India.* Berkeley: University of California Press, 1991.

Wood, Ernest. *Yoga.* Baltimore: Penguin Books, 1962.

Zelliot, Eleanor. "Bibliography on Untouchability." In *The Untouchables in Contemporary India,* edited by J. Michael Mahar. Tucson: University of Arizona Press, 1972, 431-486.

Zimmerman, Francis. "Géométrie Sociale Traditionnelle. Castes de Main Droite et Castes de Main Gauche en Inde Du Sud." *Annales Économies Sociétés Civilisations* 29 (1974): 1381-1401.

——. "Diseases of the Wind in Ayurvedic Medicine: An Ethnolinguistic Approach to Nosology and Therapeutics." *The Society for the Social History of Medicine Bulletin* 24 (1979): 26-27.

Zinkin, Taya. *Caste Today*. London: Oxford University Press, 1962.

# About the Author

Alan Dundes is professor of anthropology and folklore at the University of California, Berkeley. After earning his doctorate in folklore from Indiana University in 1962, he joined the department of anthropology at Berkeley in 1963, becoming full professor in 1968. He has devoted much of his career to applying psychoanalytic theory to the materials of folklore. Author or editor of more than thirty books, he has also written one hundred and fifty articles for professional journals. In 1993, he was awarded the Pitrè Prize: the Sigillo d'Oro (Seal of Gold) for lifetime achievement in folklore, the first American to receive this honor. Among his books are *Interpreting Folklore* (1980), *Parsing through Customs: Essays by a Freudian Folklorist* (1987), *Life Is Like a Chicken Coop Ladder: A Study of German National Character through Folklore* (1989), and *From Game to War and Other Psychoanalytic Essays on Folklore* (1997).